policy analysis and education series

DALE MANN, GENERAL EDITOR

Impact and Response

Federal Aid and State Education Agencies

MIKE M. MILSTEIN

Teachers College Press
Teachers College, Columbia University
New York, New York

Library of Congress Cataloging in Publication Data

Milstein, Mike M.
    Impact and response.

    (Policy analysis and education series)
    Bibliography: p.
    Includes index.
    1. Federal aid to education—United States.
2. State boards of education. I. Title. II. Series.
LB2825.M475   379'.121'0973   76-14887
ISBN O-8077-2502-1
ISBN 0-8077-2501-3 pbk.

Cover and book design by Angela Foote
Cover photograph by Linda Milstein
MANUFACTURED IN THE UNITED STATES OF AMERICA

To Linda, Tema, and Avi

General Editor's Introduction

Although cynics may disagree, governments do change the way they conduct their business and these changes have implications for all of us. As Professor Milstein points out in this book, federal support for education was once small-scale, short-term, and general. Then, in the 1960s, it became much larger, longer term, and *much* more specific. Now, in a reaction against categorical programs and the spectre of federal control, revenue sharing has become a reality; the federal government is returning close to $6 billion a year to 38,000 state and local governments with few strings attached and fewer questions asked. These changes come about because the public expects new, different, and hopefully better responses from all of its governments. The states and state agencies are often the focus of such expectations. Their response to a series of recent changes in educational policy is Professor Milstein's concern in this book.

The Office of Education is a single agency faced—sometimes—with 17,000 school districts: OE's 400 Maryland Avenue headquarters is a single building faced—sometimes—with the 90,000 school buildings in the United States. The logistics of that situation have convinced many observers that if the state level of government didn't exist, it would have to be invented. But the performance of the states has been so erratic that no one seems too sure about them. Among school people, states are thought to be especially important intersections between the federal source and the local target for educational funds. Thus, understanding the impact federal aid had on state departments of education can illuminate a crucial policy intersection.

One of the virtues of a federal system is that states can act as laboratories for change. They can develop and test, on a more tractable basis, the sorts of programs and policies that may later be used at the federal level. But have state departments served this role in education? Professor Milstein addresses that question in distinguishing reactive from proactive developments in state departments of education. He examines the shift from regulation to innovation, from auditing functions to leadership. Moreover, in considering how well the states handled these new responsibilities, he also illuminates the political context in which state departments of education are located. Not only are they structurally and procedurally located between federal and local pincers, their own immediate environ contains legislatures, governor's offices, competing executive agencies, elected and appointed state boards, and a welter of interest groups. Educational policy is ground out in moves made between and among those agencies, offices, and divisions.

Impact and Response is concentrated on such interorganizational relations and the dynamics of bureaucracies and their clientele. As the policy-making discretion of the states continues to grow, Professor Milstein's consideration of how these agencies have already reacted should be useful for future planning. The number of topics pressing for attention on the agenda of the states—taxation, finance, equalization of opportunity, and race—dictates that we pay careful attention to state agencies as pivotal actors in the policy process.

DALE MANN
New York City

Author's Preface

Camelot, for education, has come and gone. During the 1960s the postwar "baby boom" reached its zenith in the schools and innovative and costly instructional approaches proliferated. Building programs flourished and school budgets rocketed upward. Local property-tax payers were surprisingly receptive to calls for increasing school support; legislatures expanded the states' fiscal commitment to education; and, last but far from least, the federal government exploded onto the educational governance and support scene. These were the days when educators claimed, and others believed, that our country's educational problems could be alleviated if only sufficient dollars would be thrown at them. New ideas flourished and hopes ran high. By now most of us realize that the promises were far greater than the outcomes.

Thus far, the decade of the 1970s has been most noted for retrenchment of support for education by policy-making bodies at all levels of government. School budgets are peaking and, in many instances, are actually being cut back as local taxpayers vote down fiscal issues where they can, state legislatures turn a deaf ear to educators' entreaties to continuously raise state-aid formula ceilings, and the expansion in federal aid has reached at least a temporary plateau. Clearly it is now time to take stock. What happened? What went right and what went wrong? What lessons, if any, have we learned? In short, what has been the result of the efforts at all levels of government to improve the effectiveness of education in solving society's most plaguing problems?

The intent of this work is to explore the results of one of these efforts: the rapid and massive infusion of resources and demands by the federal government, and the role of state education agencies (SEAs) in managing those resources and satisfying those demands. SEAs were charged with overseeing the distribution and implementation of programs funded as a result of the growth in federal categorical aid. The expectations for changes in SEA structures and modifications of relationships among federal, state, and local education officials were without precedent. As the title of the book implies, the impact of the federal involvement has been great. The question remains as to how effectively the SEAs have responded to that impact. Sufficient time has now passed to justify exploration of this question. It should be done, nonal governance today and the possibilities for tomorrow.

In all likelihood SEAs will continue to play a key role in educational governance, if for no other reason than because they occupy a central location in our federal system. Therefore it is hoped that this work will provide educators and others who wish to comprehend educational policy-making with a clearer understanding of the nature of intergovernmental decision making in education and the SEAs' capacity to respond to their changing environment.

Drawing upon studies of SEAs that have been carried out both by the writer and by other students of this phenomenon, the contents focus on the SEAs' responsiveness to recent federal aid programs, especially the National Defense Education Act of 1958 and the Elementary and Secondary Education Act of 1965. Chapter I sets the scene by establishing an historical view of educational governance in the United States, placing particular emphasis on the evolution of the states' role, the growth of the SEAs, and the shifts in federal involvement from the founding of the nation until now. Chapter II provides frameworks for thinking about the process of educational governance and the place of SEAs in that process. The frameworks include a perception of policy development and a systems view of SEA activities in the implementation of established policies. Based on these frameworks, Chapters III, IV, and V explore SEA intraorganizational and interorganizational activities as these agencies geared up to administer federal aid programs. These chapters bring together much of what we know about the impact of federal aid on SEAs. Chapter VI brings the strands of the presentation together and posits some probable directions for the future.

Thanks are due to many individuals for their contributions to this effort, but there are a few whose interest, insights, and efforts were particularly useful. Special appreciation is felt for the long-term support of Edgar Morphet, including his help in finding funds for research, his encouragement when things looked most bleak, and his critical commentary when it was most needed. Dr. Morphet, professor emeritus at the University of California at Berkeley and former director of Improving State Leadership in Education, a federally funded organization that, among other things, sponsored studies of state educational governance, has given most unselfishly of his severely limited time in support of this effort. Others, including Robert Jennings of the State University of New York at Buffalo, and Harry Gray and John Davies, both of the North East London Polytechnic's Anglian Regional Management Centre, provided improvements to the book by their thoughtful readings of the manuscript.

I am also most grateful to Dale Mann of Teachers College, Columbia University, who, as general editor of this series, demonstrated extensive patience with the procrastinations and whims of the writer and so willingly offered useful advice as the book moved from a raw pile of data to the finished manuscript. Finally, the work would never have been completed if it had not been for the typing skills and tolerance of Ellen Kalway, Diana Wignall, and Gladys Phillips. Of course, the misthoughts and unclarities that may remain in the book are, in spite of the good efforts of all of these individuals, the sole responsibility of the writer.

MIKE M. MILSTEIN
Buffalo, New York

Contents

Figures

Impact and Response

I/Roles of the States and the Federal Government in Education

Educational governance is in a state of flux. In the past educators and others interested in the public education sector could say with relative assurance that they knew how the system worked and "who was in charge." Today there is less certainty. At the school district level, teachers have used negotiations to become a force while citizens' groups have become increasingly active in harassing policy makers who persist in carrying out programs these groups do not favor. At the state level, legislatures and governors have geared up to play a major role in setting priorities for education. This is due to public treasuries shrinking as public needs expand, and to the rampant divisiveness that exists among educational interest groups. At the federal level, Congress has launched major programs to achieve specific educational objectives it believes are in the country's interest. The expansion of federal aid to education has peaked temporarily but it is likely that there will be pressure to increase the federal contribution in the future.

Inevitably these increasing pressures at all levels of educational governance have challenged those within the system to adjust to new realities or face the prospect of becoming superfluous or even being dismantled and replaced by more effective structures. In short, we are witnessing a time of great uncertainty. Traditional patterns of control are being seriously strained as new forces move onto center stage. There is little question that the status quo has been unfrozen, but what the dynamics of the new patterns will eventually be are far from certain.

1

While the present situation may be unsettling for those who prefer the security of knowing how things get done, it does provide unprecedented opportunities to look at the inner workings of educational organizations* under stress. When there is little or no challenge from the outside, organizations tend to carry on business as usual and it is difficult to uncover the dynamics of organizational behavior. Routines function so smoothly that outsiders cannot easily discover critical processes and events. When organizations must adjust to unprecedented pressures from without, the normally established bureaucratic interactions, often subterranean, become more perceptible and low-level maintenance activities give way to system survival. At such times, as Thompson has noted, "Uncertainty appears as the fundamental problem for complex organizations, and coping with uncertainty, as the essence of the administrative process."[1] Thus, exploring educational organizations as they respond to stresses from without provides an opportunity to gain insights not ascertainable when relationships are more regular.

Educational governance has, over time, been noted more for stability, or even rigidity, than for uncertainty. The growing literature regarding this phenomenon at the school and school district levels indicates that change comes very slowly, if at all.[2] What has held true in the past may not, however, hold true for the future. If the many forces impinging upon education maintain their pressure, (and there is every indication that this pressure will not only be maintained but in all likelihood will increase) it will become more difficult for those within governing structures to rule unchallenged. Thus it is relevant to ask such questions as: Where are the policy-making centers in education? What are their relative strengths? How do established educational governing bodies respond to challenges? How effective are their strategies? What can we expect for the future? To answer these questions we must study the changing nature of federal-state-local relationships in education. Such explorations can help to clarify the major intergovernmental trends and intraorganizational dynamics in educational organizations that have resulted from these changing relationships.

The present work focuses on the impact of the federal government's increasing role in educational finance and policy making in the United States. Of particular interest is the manner in which the established overseers of educational governance, the state education agencies (SEAs),* have adjusted to this new and important chal-

---

*State Education Agencies will be abbreviated to SEAs throughout the book.

lenge. To establish the setting, in this chapter we will explore the role of the states in education, the historical growth of the SEAs, growth and shifts of emphases in federal aid, and the impact that this aid has had on the SEAs in recent time.

The States' Role in Education

Education has, by default, been a responsibility of the states since the founding of our nation. After deliberating the appropriate roles of the levels of government in our federal system, the delegates to the Constitutional Convention, in their wisdom, left the maintenance of education to the states. This was accomplished by simply omitting specific mention of education in the final draft of the Constitution of 1787. This delegation of responsibility to the states became somewhat more specific in 1791 with Article X of the Bill of Rights, which holds that "powers not delegated to the United States by the Constitution nor prohibited by it to the States, are reserved to the States respectively, or to the people."

The states, in turn, chose to interpret their roles in quite a limited fashion. In effect they passed the financial burden for educating the citizenry onto local communities, reserving only the rudiments of regulatory oversight for state government. Thus in most states, for the first several decades following the founding of the nation, the burden for financing and providing common schools fell on local communities with little or no financial contribution from the state. As long as the task of schooling remained relatively simple and limited in scope this arrangement seemed to suffice. But by the early 1800s the situation began to change and the states found themselves pushed toward an extended and continuing role in educational governance. In fact, as Wirt and Kirst note, "by 1820 . . . thirteen of the twenty states had developed constitutional provisions for education. The position of chief state school officer . . . had emerged in some states in 1836, and by 1870 most states provided for them; and state boards of education appeared about the same time."[3]

Initially the states moved into the vacuum by regularizing and standardizing educational performance. Over time the states have expanded their regulatory oversight to encompass audits of income and expenditures, maintenance of attendance records, establishment and policing of building codes, certification of personnel, mandatory curricular offerings, and, in some instances, development of specific courses and selection of textbooks for use in the schools.

FIGURE 1.   PERCENT OF SCHOOL REVENUES

Year	From federal sources	From state sources	From local sources
1919-20	0.3	13.8	85.9
1929-30	0.4	16.9	82.7
1939-40	1.8	30.3	68.0
1959-60	2.9	39.8	57.3
1960-61	3.8	39.8	56.4
1961-62	4.3	38.7	56.9
1962-63	3.6	39.3	57.1
1963-64	4.4	39.3	56.4
1964-65	3.8	39.7	56.5
1965-66	7.9	39.1	53.0
1966-67	7.9	39.1	53.0
1967-68	8.8	38.5	52.3
1968-69	7.4	40.0	52.6
1969-70	7.2	40.9	51.8
1970-71	7.2	40.0	52.8
1971-72	9.0	37.0	54.0

Source: National Education Association and U.S. Office of Education, as compiled by the Congressional Quarterly, *Education for a Nation,* Washington, D.C., 1972, p. 9.

Providing only marginal financial support until the end of the nineteenth century, the states have since come to carry a significant percentage of annual school costs. Figure 1 shows the contribution of federal-state-local resources for the support of public education over the past half century. Note that both the state and federal shares have increased dramatically. The states' input, as a percent of total costs, grew substantially prior to World War Two, while the federal input has had its most dramatic growth more recently.

Growth of the SEAs

The National Education Association's comprehensive history of educational development in the United States[4] indicates that the SEAs have consistently been given low priority by governors and legislators. Although many SEAs were established in the nineteenth century, most existed in name only.[5] Even where SEA chief school-officers were retained, few if any resources were provided to permit them to plan for the improvement of education in their states. Some states, particularly in New England, employed chief state school-officers on a full-time basis, but most left the administration of SEAs to other state officials who handled this task on an ad hoc, part-time basis. Even in those states where state education superintendents existed, long-range planning suffered because these men frequently had to hold a second position to earn an adequate living. Further-more, they had to spend the vast majority of their time at activities such as direct supervision of teachers, which minimized their op-portunities to play a leadership role in education. There was not great potential in their roles anyway; since state legislatures and governors had not yet accepted responsibility for providing a mini-mum level of educational finances for public elementary and sec-ondary education, there was very little for these men to plan. Most SEAs, with little if any funds to regulate and very limited talent available, were hard pressed to simply collect and store basic educa-tional data. In summary, most SEAs entered the twentieth century as undernourished and relatively isolated agencies of state government.

To complicate matters, as cities grew in the early part of this century, school officials from these urban areas set out to develop independent relationships with state legislatures. In most cases ur-ban districts afforded more attractive and more remunerative careers for educators than did SEAs. Therefore, it is not surprising that city systems frequently tended to look disparagingly upon SEA supervi-sion. This left SEAs with constituencies composed, in large part, of rural school districts. With the urbanization and suburbanization of the states, this has meant a continuously dwindling power base for the SEAs.

In the last several decades major shifts in educational gover-nance have occurred providing SEAs with enormously increased potential to influence the course of education in their states. Increas-ing fiscal responsibility and regulatory activity at the state level have had the most noticeable impacts. In California for example, average daily attendance increased by 66% between 1948 and 1957. But during this same period the state's contribution to the support of public schools increased by 147%, the SEA's staff increased by 88%, and its expenditures increased by 165%.[6] Thus, even before the present expansion of federal aid to education, the role of the states in educational governance had begun to grow markedly. As we shall see though, the expansion of federal programs led to an accelerating rate of SEA activity that has exceeded all expectations.

Today activities vary greatly across the several SEAs, depending primarily upon the preferences of these agencies' leadership and the expectations of legislatures and governors. However, to one degree or another, all SEAs seem to be expected to fulfill these major requirements, as summarized by Friedman:

1. *To Advise* state government on the conditions which government should require and should expect to prevail within the statewide educational system, and on the public policies, priorities, standards, criteria, and actions needed to produce those conditions.
2. *To Ascertain* whether the conditions stipulated by state government actually are being met by each school, school system, or other entity within the State Education Agency's purview.
3. *To Assure,* by taking suitable actions, that unsatisfactory conditions are corrected wherever and whenever they are found to exist.[7]

As shall be argued throughout the book, "to assure" is often easier to say than to do; government agencies such as SEAs are limited in their capacity "to assure" that conditions will be improved. Such factors as limited resources, variations in expectations (especially when more than one governmental level is involved in the action), and insufficient staff—both in size and ability—make this an impossibility.

The Federal Role

The states have been left with primary responsibility for educating the citizenry, but there has always been a federal "interest" in education. This may sound contradictory to the intent of the Constitution, but it makes a great deal of sense when one considers that *all* levels of government in our federal system serve, cooperatively, the needs and demands of the nation. That is, tasks overlap; they can never be neatly divided. Local, state, and federal levels of government cannot function in isolation from each other. As Grodzins has vividly reminded us, our federal system is analogous to a marble cake:

Wherever you slice through it you reveal an inseparable mixture of differently colored ingredients. There is no neat horizontal stratification. Vertical and diagonal lines almost obliterate the horizontal ones, and in some places there are unexpected whirls and an imperceptible merging of colors, so that it is difficult to tell where one ends and the other begins. So it is with federal, state and local responsibility in the chaotic marble cake of American government.[8]

Still, there are those who argue that the federal government should have no role in education because of the limitations of the Tenth Amendment. Since the Constitution makes no reference to education, they conclude that any responsibility for education must rest, by default, with the states.

Advocates of federal aid have championed the "general welfare" clause (Article I, Section 8) of the Constitution, which declares that the "Congress shall have the power to lay and collect taxes, duties, imposts and excises, to pay the debts and provide for the common defense and general welfare of the United States." Liberally interpreted, this implies that Congress has the power to spend for any purpose it deems necessary for the general welfare of the nation. As Scribner has noted, "The 'general welfare clause,' although a subject for much debate over the years since the Constitution was established, provides the basis for the increasingly large amounts of federal spending in education."[9] Furthermore, as Elazar concludes, spending has been a continuous intergovernmental feature in our federal system:

> Co-operative federalism—the patterned sharing of governmental activities by all levels of government—has been characteristic of the American federal system since its establishment. American governments have traditionally assumed responsibilities only in response to public demands but, where governments have acted, federal, state, and local governments usually have acted in concert. Whether this "co-operative federalism" was intended by the founders of the Union or not, it was quickly demonstrated to be necessary.[10]

Close examination of the history of federal involvement in the educational pursuits of the states reveals a movement away from the strict constructionists' viewpoint and toward an increasing investment of funds and ever-widening interest in the scope, aims, and outcomes of educational programs by the federal government. Furthermore, recurring throughout the history of federal aid to education has been one constant theme: each federal contribution to the states' educational efforts has been granted to advance national objectives. The following brief discussion of the stages of federal involvement in education should underscore this point.

A History of Federal Aid to Education: Five Stages

STAGE ONE. The national government indicated its interest in the educational functions of the states even before the Constitution was enacted. Under the Articles of Confederation, Congress passed the Survey Ordinance of 1785, which states that there "shall be reserved the lot number 16 of every township for the maintenance of public schools in each township." Two years later the Northwest Ordinance of 1787 repeated this provision, declaring "Religion, morality and knowledge, being necessary to good government and the happiness of mankind, schools and the means of education shall be forever encouraged."

The dimension of these grants, which encouraged the development of national lands, continued to increase until 1896 when Utah was granted four sections of every township for public school maintenance. In all, 30 states were ceded more than 80 million acres of land as a result of these grants. The funds gained from the sale of these lands were to be put into permanent school endowments, but only a small percentage of these resources were captured for these endowments because the money was poorly managed. In this instance some minimal federal regulation might well have benefited the states. Such regulation would not have interferred with the states' prerogative to determine curriculum, administer schools, or exercise their legitimate powers in any form, but it might have done much to curb the excessive abuses that curtailed the potential support for educational needs.

STAGE TWO. The second stage of federal aid began when Congress passed the Morrill Act of 1862. This act supported the expansionist tendencies of the northern states by establishing land grant colleges. The land involved was to be used for "endowment, support, and maintenance of at least one college where the leading object shall be, without excluding other scientific and classical studies, and including military tactics, to teach such branches of learning as are related to agriculture and the mechanic arts . . . ." Although the act was the first instance of a federal grant for specific educational purposes, it did not exclude the teaching of other subjects. Most important, it illustrated that the federal government could and would take action when it believed the states were not training a manpower base sufficient to meet national needs.

In both the first and second stages, the federal government granted federal lands on a one-time-only basis, and in neither instance did it contribute funds.[11]

STAGE THREE. The third stage was inspired by the decreasing flow of skilled craftsmen immigrating to this country and by the United States involvement in World War I. Once more the federal government showed its ability to stimulate educational activity, in this case through passage of the Smith-Hughes Act of 1917, which encouraged schools to promote programs leading to immediate gainful employment.

The Smith-Hughes Act, which provided matching funds for vocational education in agriculture, the trades and industry, and the homemaking arts, added three new dimensions to federal grants for education:

1. It was the first categorical grant. That is, it was the first grant made to attain specified outcomes. (The Morrill Act encouraged certain curricular offerings, but did not limit land grant institutions to these pursuits).
2. It was the first grant to be administered by the SEAs. In fact, until the late 1950s the Smith-Hughes Act and subsequent vocational appropriations measures that modified it through the next 40 years, was the *only* experience SEAs had regarding federal grant administration.
3. It was the first grant for which the states had to commit their own funds. Smith-Hughes called for "matching" federal-state financial input. This feature remained as a standard federal procedure until quite recently.

There is substantial evidence that the act did stimulate the states to greater efforts in vocational education. For example the act calls for equal matching, but by 1960 the "typical state provided from state and local sources five times as much financial support for vocational education as the federal vocational grants."[12] The act, with its several amendments, stands as the longest continuous federal grant to states for educational purposes.

STAGE FOUR. The fourth stage of federal involvement in education grew out of the impact of the depression of the 1930s when education programs were established to serve national goals of relief and recovery. Among the many educationally related federal programs were the Civilian Conservation Corps (1933), the Federal Emergency Relief Administration (1933), the Public Works Administration (1933), the National Youth Administration (1935), and finally, the Federal Surplus Commodities Corporation (1935), which led to the National School Lunch Act of 1946. Emergency legislation was extended during World War II with the Lanham Act

(1941), which provided financial assistance to school districts in areas where federal activities such as military bases created a financial burden. In 1950 Public Laws 815 and 874 extended this aid and made the so-called Impacted Areas Program a continuing federal commitment.

While the earlier grants left complete program control to the states, these latter grants increasingly involved the federal government in decisions concerning the use of federal funds. By the end of the fourth stage it was becoming clear that the federal government's activities would include involvement in educational decision making along with the granting of federal dollars.

STAGE FIVE. The present stage of federal participation in education began as the United States emerged from World War II.[13] In education, as in most domestic areas, federal spending increased greatly. In addition, the form of federal grants changed from temporary, special-purpose needs to programs noted for their permanent institutional characteristics. From 1945 to 1952 the largest percentage of funds was to aid veterans' education, but in the last two decades funding efforts have been channeled into programs that are expected to be continuously renewed, such as the National Defense Education Act (1958), the Vocational Education Act (1963), the Elementary and Secondary Education Act (1965), and the Education Professions Development Act (1968).

Congress attempts to assure that national objectives will be met[14] by "appropriating funds for special purposes and requiring that those funds be spent for those purposes."[15] This has been especially true during the last decade: "Between 1960 and 1970 the basic character of the typical federal assistance program changed from helping state or local governments accomplish *their objectives* with perfunctory general federal review, to using state governments as an *administrative convenience* under some explicit controls for accomplishing specific federal objectives."[16]

The federal government significantly increased its total financial commitment to education during this stage (from approximately $50 million in 1945 to more than $2.5 billion in 1970) at the same time it altered its objectives for educational funding. In little more than a decade, the federal government has initiated a number of programs pursuant to these objectives. Major programs that directly affect elementary and secondary education include:

A. *The Cooperative Research Act of 1954* (Public Law 83-531). Authorized the U.S. Commissioner of Education to make contracts with SEAs and higher education institutions to conduct research and demonstrations in education. This act did much to interest researchers in exploring educationally-related problems.

B. *The National Defense Education Act of 1958* (Public Law 85-864). A reaction to the apparent headstart of the Soviet Union in the exploration of outer space as well as a response to domestic shifts in knowledge and technology needs, this program promotes the improvement of educational programs in specific subject areas. Included are provisions for assistance to students in higher education preparing to be teachers; matching grants to states, and through the states, to public schools (and loans to private schools) to purchase equipment required in science, mathematics, and modern foreign languages (later extended to other subject areas); graduate fellowships; support for testing, guidance, and counseling; grants to colleges for modern foreign language in-service training programs and to elementary and secondary teachers for taking such courses; and grants for research into teaching aids such as television, radio, and motion pictures.

C. *The Manpower Development and Training Act of 1962* (Public Law 87-415). This program, supporting public school vocational education for adults, is specifically geared to train or retrain unemployed and underemployed workers. The concern of the federal government is with the effects of automation and technological changes in the economy. The program makes a concerted effort to assess manpower needs and translate them into vocational programs in the schools.

D. *The Vocational Education Act of 1963* (Public Law 88-210). This act, which increased federal support for vocational education fourfold, is meant to improve existing vocational education and develop new programs to train youth for gainful employment in the light of actual or anticipated opportunities. The Appalachian Regional Development Act of 1965, geared to the special needs of that area, is an extension of this act.

E. *The Economic Opportunity Act of 1964* (Public Law 88-452). A multi-fronted attack on poverty until former President Nixon withheld funds, this act affected the schools from preschool through adult education. The only segment of this program that has been directly administered by the United States Office of Education (OE)* of the Department of Health, Education, and Welfare is adult basic education. Because until 1973 most of the programs were administered by the Office of Economic Opportunity, an independent federal agency, the act has required cooperation of school officials with other community leaders, an almost unique phenomenon in educational policy making.

*The United States Office of Education will be abbreviated to OE throughout the book.

F. *The Elementary and Secondary Education Act of 1965* (Public
Law 89-10). This program, the most massive of the current crop of
federal inputs, focuses primarily on meeting the needs of the educationally disadvantaged. Over a billion dollars—with no matching requirements—are allocated through the major provision (Title
I) to provide educational programs geared particularly to the needs
of children who come from low-income families. Other titles include grants for school libraries; grants for the development of
"supplementary educational centers" to provide services otherwise not sufficiently available; grants for research and development programs; and grants to SEAs to strengthen their planning
capacities and help them establish the major educational needs in
their states. This act has consistently been funded to a level of at
least $1.5 billion.

G. *The Education Professions Development Act of 1967* (Public Law
90-35). The EDPA's purpose is "to improve the quality of teaching
and to help meet critical shortages of adequately trained educational personnel." The program includes resources for needs assessments, training and retraining teachers, and upgrading higher
education programs that provide training for teachers.

Over the almost two hundred years of federal involvement in
education, the focus has shifted dramatically from short-term and
relatively general support programs to long-term and highly specific
programs. Whether one criticizes or supports this growing federal
role, it is certain that there has been an impact. Furthermore, the
most recent stage of federal involvement seems to have been particularly relevant to the ills of twentieth-century urban life. As Norman
Drachler, former superintendent of schools in Detroit, has noted:

Our plight would have been much more serious had it not been for . . .
the stimulus that federal legislation gave to our schools. Federal partic-
ipation in education has:
  Highlighted the shortcomings of the schools,
  Focused attention on the education of the poor,
  Stimulated participation by parents,
  Stressed accountability,
  Provided through teacher and community agents and other mem-
    bers of the community a new dimension to the educational pro-
    fession,
  Encouraged and supported multi-cultural and bilingual programs,
    and
  Fostered and encouraged change and innovation in our schools.[17]

In short, as Drachler emphasizes, federal aid has been a telling force in moving education. The question remains, however, whether SEAs have been able to make the necessary changes and upgrade their ability to participate in this process.

Federal Aid and the Growth of SEAs

The largest percentage of federal aid to schools has been channeled through the SEAs on the assumption that "the state provides a broader base for educational leadership and planning than is possible at the local level, yet one which is far closer to the local school, or to the local college than the federal government."[18] Thus as the federal role gathered momentum in the 1950s and the 1960s, OE, the federal government's executive agency responsible for federally funded education programs, turned increasingly to the SEAs to assure that the intent of education programs would be achieved.

The support given to the SEAs to accomplish their tasks is impressive. Although the federal share of educational financing presently stands at less than 9% of the total financial input to public elementary and secondary education (amounting by 1970 to only $22 to $50 per child, or 3% to 10% of school district budgets[19]), the ratio of fiscal input to the SEAs is substantially greater. In 1970 the SEAs spent about $300 million for salaries, contracted services, equipment, and other expenses. Of this total the federal government contributed about $120 million, which constituted more than 40% of SEA expenditures.[20] These figures, however, do not provide an accurate measure of the total impact of federal programs on the SEAs. As one OE report points out, it is "quite evident that there are few employees of State departments of education who are not in some way touched by one or more federal programs. In many of the smaller states there are almost as many federal programs and service areas that could draw upon the resources of state departments of education as there are professional employees* in these departments."[21] In short, although their salaries may not be supported by federal resources, virtually all SEA personnel find themselves involved in some way with federal program-management activities.

For most SEAs the bulk of staff increases in the past two decades has been due to the availability of federal resources. For exam-

---

*OE, in this report, defined a professional position as one "requiring at least a baccalaureate or first professional degree conferred by an accredited institution of higher education."

ple, the California SEA, which received 35% of its total operating funds from the federal government in 1970 (about 5% *below* the national average), drew special attention from that state's legislative analyst, who reported to the state legislature that in 1962 there were only 93 federally funded positions in the department but by 1968 this number had grown to 454 (representing an increase of almost 400%). During this same period positions supported by state dollars increased from 575 to 669 (representing an increase of only about 16%).[22]

Quantitative increases tell only part of the story. The federal government has also proven its ability to influence the manner of deployment of staff in SEAs. For example, the NDEA originally specified mathematics, science, modern foreign languages, and guidance as the only authorized subject areas that could be supported under the act. Just one year after this program was launched, the U.S. Commissioner of Education was able to conclude that "State education agencies have nearly tripled their staffs of supervisor-specialists in Science, Mathematics, modern foreign languages and guidance and counseling since the passage of the act."[23]

It is important to note that the impact differs among the states. This is due to variance in such factors as size of the SEAs before the current federal input, their aggressiveness in seeking federal funds and the states' incidence of need according to federal guidelines. In fact the rate of increase in staff recruitment varied significantly among SEAs during the hectic years of the 1960s when federal programs such as the NDEA and the ESEA were having their greatest initial impact. A sample of nine states over these years (see Figure 2) indicates a substantial range of SEA staff growth, from a low of 54% in Minnesota to a high of 226% in Alabama. The greatest increases seem to have come in states where the fewest staff were employed at the start of the 1960s, but there is no simple linear relationship. Note, for example, in Figure 2 the growth in the Rhode Island and Alabama SEAs.

Five SEAs received less than 22% of their operating revenues from federal support during 1970—South Carolina, Hawaii, North Carolina, New York, and Illinois. On the other end of the continuum five SEAs received more than 68% of their operating revenues from federal support during 1970—Mississippi, Arizona, Texas, New Hampshire, and Idaho.[24] In short, the level of federal input as contrasted to the level of state input for SEAs varies enormously, but there is no distinct geographical pattern to the level of support.

Thus, while the federal input has resulted in impressive in-

FIGURE 2.   STAFF SIZE AND GROWTH IN NINE SEAS, 1962-1968

State	Professional Personnel 1962	Professional Personnel 1968	Percent Increase
Minnesota	100	154	54
Texas	173	300	73
Rhode Island	35	61	74
New York	277	557	101
Utah	38	77	103
Vermont	29	73	152
New Jersey	69	197	186
South Dakota	19	58	205
Alabama	43	140	226

Source: Abstracted from the Fourth Annual Report of the Advisory Council on State Departments of Education, *The State of State Departments of Education,* (Washington D.C., U.S. Government Printing Office, 1969), pp. 14-31.

creases in the number of personnel in SEAs, there have been options retained at the state level. Whether emanating from within the SEAs or from policy-making bodies such as state legislatures, the growth patterns in the SEAs have been influenced by decisions taken at the state level. These preferences clearly differ from state to state, so making sweeping generalizations about the impact of federal aid on SEAs is inappropriate.

Still, it is true that during the 1960s and into the 1970s the increasing quantity of federal funds and the expanding number of federal programs have created enormous organizational problems for all SEAs, many of which have more than doubled their personnel and operating budgets since these programs were initiated. Such an infusion of fiscal and human resources is bound to require pervasive organizational adjustments. This holds true for each of the levels of educational governance. OE, for example, has undergone several major reorganizations as its role was vastly expanded by recent federal programs.[25]

There is some doubt that the SEAs will be able to employ these new resources to their advantage. In fact, there is reason to believe that most SEAs may resist taking the initiative required to best employ them. As Haskew has noted:

There are chief state school officers who have proved extremely agile in linking federal programs with state interests. But there are also observers who prophesy that, in light of such developments, the state department of education is destined for a career as an executive branch of the "Federal Establishment" for education.[26]

Given the potential for differing response patterns it becomes important to explore strategies pursued by SEAs. Federal aid has set up "a test of each state government and its state education agency. The question pending is whether the states are up to the task of bringing about the changes."[27] It is hoped that this work can provide some light concerning SEA responses to the federal input so that educators and other interested parties can better understand the evolving status and roles of the local, state, and federal governments in educational governance. It should also lead to a clearer perception of the dynamics of organizational change, providing insight into the means by which complex organizations seek to achieve control over their own destiny *vis-a-vis* influencers in their environments.

The remainder of the book is divided into five chapters. Chapter II presents a conceptualization of the dynamics of federal-state relations and describes the data bases for the discussion that follows. Chapters III and IV explore the tasks pursued by SEAs, particularly as they have been modified to meet the challenges of federal program administration. Chapter V looks closely into the ways that SEAs have dealt with their ever-more complex environments while attempting to maintain control over their own activities. Finally, Chapter VI, employing the conceptual framework introduced in Chapter II, provides a summation and explores probable futures as federal inputs continue to alter the face of educational governance.

II/A View of the SEAs in the Policy-Making Process

Educational policy making is a complex process. In part this is because many individuals and groups take part in it, but it is also because educational policies are established at all three levels of our federal system. In the early years of our nation, local communities made practically all decisions required to maintain the schools. But by the opening of the twentieth century, support for education had become an endeavor shared between the states and communities. Today, as the federal government moves into educational governance, the process becomes even more complex and less predictable. Chapter II focuses on several tasks. First, the educational policy-making process will be explored to gain a perspective about the organizations, particularly the SEAs, that must implement policy. Second, a systems framework will be introduced as a vehicle, which will be used throughout the book, to examine policy implementation by the SEAs. Finally, the field work and related studies that underlie the work will be described.

The Evolution of Policy

Policy making in the public sector can be viewed as a process that usually unfolds in a fairly predictable series of stages through which desired changes move. This path is fraught with risks and only a small fraction of contending preferences emerge as law.[1]

The process originates with a *period of dissatisfaction*. At this point an identifiable group of people who share important characteristics, such as the aged, laborers, women, or minorities, finds itself dissatisfied with its lot. The dissatisfaction may be due to the existence of repressive policies: for example, pay scales and job oppor-

FIGURE 3. THE POLICY-MAKING PROCESS

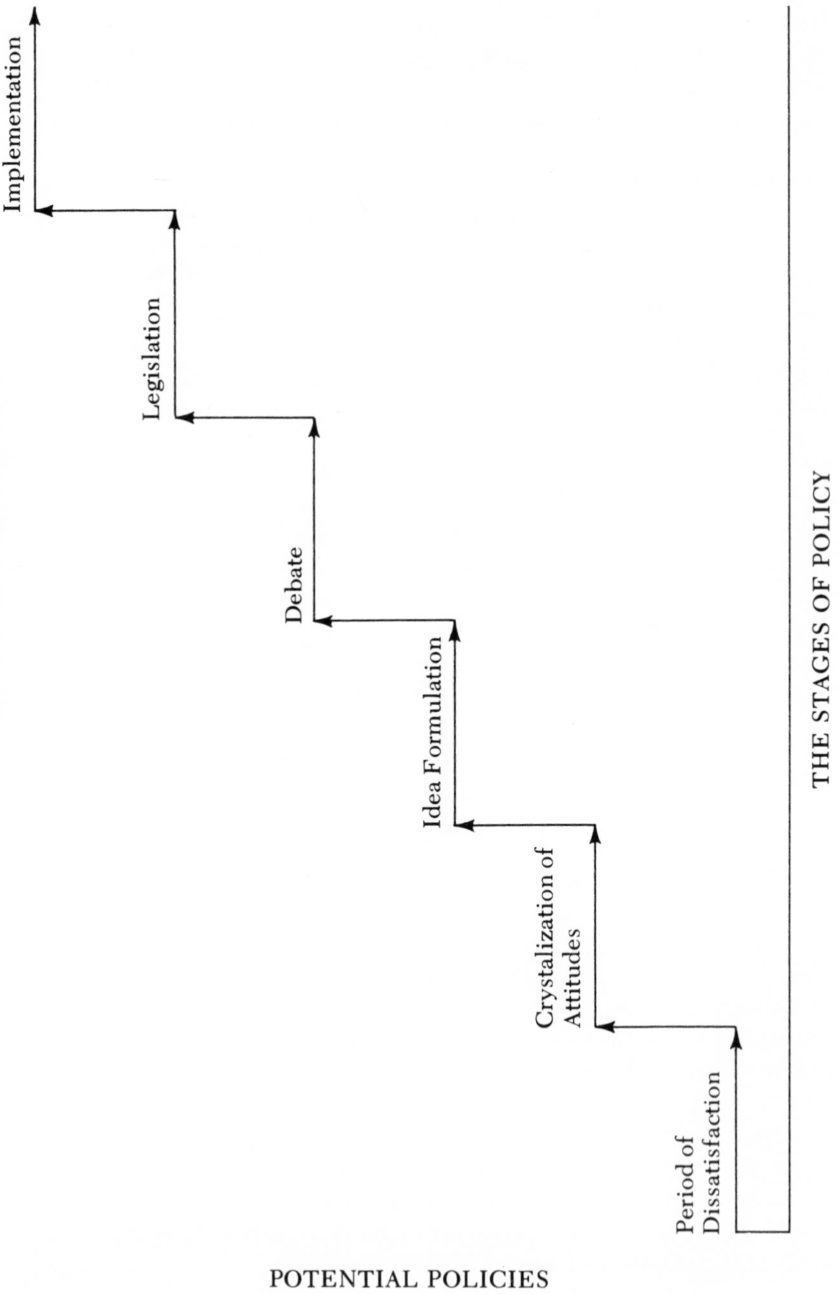

Implementation

Legislation

Debate

Idea Formulation

Crystalization of Attitudes

Period of Dissatisfaction

THE STAGES OF POLICY

POTENTIAL POLICIES

tunities may discriminate against women. It may also be due to the lack of policies that would improve their lot: for example, there may be need for government regulation and support of health care centers for geriatric patients.

If the dissatisfaction is intense and of sufficient longevity a *crystalization of attitudes* begins to occur. At this stage group identity sharpens, grievances begin to acquire clarity, and attitudes about the dissatisfaction start to focus. Leaders emerge to articulate the group's grievances so that its members, and others, fully understand the nature of the grievance. For example, recall how in the early 1960s civil rights leaders such as Martin Luther King emerged to rally both blacks and whites in a major effort to crystalize the feelings of the long-oppressed black minority. Those who took part in or even closely observed the march on Selma, Alabama, and the massive gathering at the Lincoln Monument in Washington are well aware of the importance of this rallying stage.

If attitude crystalization is successful, a period of time follows that is dominated by *idea formulation*. At this stage dissatisfactions are translated into proposed alternatives viewed by group members as better than the existing situation. These alternatives tend to emerge out of the dialogue carried on during the preceeding stage. For example, the civil rights movement shifted from the vague declarations of inequality that predominated during the attitude-crystalization stage to much more specific ideas packaged as demands for equal educational opportunities, elimination of discrimination in public places, and the easing of franchise restrictions, particularly in the South, so that the polling booth could be used to give blacks an opportunity to participate in public decisions.

The ideas that emerge usually encompass a diversity of views so that they will be broad enough to meet the expectations of most rank-and-file group members. Furthermore, they often include inputs from diverse combinations of group members, informal and formal group leaders, and others from outside the group who are enlisted for this creative process. The only overriding consideration is that the ideas must be viewed by group members as alternatives around which they can rally.

With a platform of ideas established, the leaders next move beyond their own group to convince influential individuals, groups, and organizations that their platform is legitimate and timely. This *debate stage* serves two important purposes. First, it incorporates needed modifications, providing an opportunity to test the potential reception of specific policy demands. Reactions from both friends and foes provide group leaders with feedback so they can incorporate necessary substantive and political modifications in the policy proposals that will ultimately be presented to the appropriate policy-making body.* For example, civil rights groups wishing to have integration policies approved often first test out their ideas on both pro-integration and anti-integration groups so they can devise proposals that meet major criticisms *before* they present them to school boards. Through this debate process civil rights groups have learned that middle-class whites will often accept integration if it occurs gradually, but will resist if it takes place rapidly. Many of the more successful integration programs are those that promote "phased" integration (e.g., integrating a single grade annually, usually starting with kindergarten).

Second, as a result of testing ideas, the base of active involvement is often widened. The dissatisfied group often picks up unanticipated supporters who can be enlisted to publicize the cause by such means as door-to-door canvases, telegrams to legislators, and coffee hours and parties at which group representatives can speak.

The ideas that survive such public debate are then clarified, often approved by the group membership, and put in the appropriate form for presentation to a policy-making body at the *legislative stage*. Members of policy-making bodies are petitioned by representatives of the dissatisfied group to adopt their platform as a rule or law within its domain of control. Members of these policy-making bodies follow public debate closely so it is possible that they may have already formed positions about the ideas being put forward. Those who indicate their support of the petitioning group's position are often requested to lend it a degree of respectability and legitimacy by sponsoring the group's legislative proposals. The dynamics at the legislative stage center around maximizing the potential of moving proposals through a complex and often alien policy-making terrain to the ultimate approval by the members of that body.

Those few policy proposals surviving this treacherous process to be granted the status of rule or law must then be *implemented*. Of course, the process is far from static. Even those few policies that

---

*The term "policy-making body" applies equally to any and all legally recognized policy groups at the federal, state, county, and local levels of government. Thus for example the term could refer to Congress, a state legislature, a county education board, or a local school board.

survive often find themselves open to challenge. The process can begin anew if other groups view the new policy as putting them at a disadvantage. But let us assume that the newly approved policy is sufficiently acceptable to most of the interested parties and is ready for implementation. At this point there is much that leaders of executive agencies can do to either enforce the law as it stands or to modify its impact. What they do depends greatly on how they interpret the new policy, which in turn, is tempered both by their judgment of the "goodness" of the policy and how they view their roles in the enforcement process.

The values and administrative behavior preferences of executive-agency leaders are potent factors in the ultimate fate of approved policies. As an example, recall how many school boards and administrators charged with carrying out racial integration after the Supreme Court's *Brown vs. Board of Education* decision in 1954 sought ways to evade their responsibilities or stall the inevitable by fighting the issue in the courts. Often these tactics were dictated by white school boards that held values at variance with those of the Supreme Court. At other times school officials resisted racial integration rather than develop difficult and complex programs—or contend with political difficulties—to meet the Court's demands. They did so because their administrative behavior preferences led them to the conclusion that it would be safer to maintain segregation than to proceed upon the risky path toward integration. In contrast, the United States Attorney General's Office under Robert F. Kennedy, which accepted the intent of the Supreme Court's ruling, vigorously prosecuted public and private organizations resisting implementation of both that ruling and the several civil rights laws passed by Congress. Not only did Kennedy and his aides agree with the values underlying these policies, they also practiced aggressive administrative behavior. The two together—shared values and aggressive administrative behavior—resulted in active prosecution of those who tried to subvert civil rights policies.

In short, executive agencies can choose to abide by the intent of the law or attempt to subvert it. If an agency is dominated by officers who oppose the purposes of a policy, or react defensively by seeking to placate rather than innovate and take risks, there will probably be very little agency thrust to see that policies are vigorously implemented. In contrast, if an agency charged with policy implementation is led by administrators who agree with the purposes of a policy and/or prefer to do battle with groups that obstruct desired changes, it will be involved in many controversies and probably obtain more extensive results.

The point is that executive agencies, at any level of government, can do much to subvert, modify, uphold, or even expand the intent of rules and laws. What they choose to do is highly dependent on their leaders' attitudes about particular policies and their perceptions of "appropriate" administrative behavior. Top-level officers in these agencies set an example for those who must carry out tasks internally. They also maintain frequent relations with interest-group leaders, policy-making bodies, and key officers in other executive agencies, both at their governmental level and from other levels of the federal system. They can choose to capitalize upon these relationships to facilitate the implementation of policies, or respond minimally to challenges or even hinder implementation.

Thus the role of executive agencies in the implementation of law is crucial. It is this role that we will explore in detail, especially as it pertains to the activities of the SEAs in implementing federal education programs.

The Dynamics of Implementing Policy

When a policy is finally approved and ready to be implemented by the appropriate executive agency, there will be several groups that find cause to watch over with some vigilance that agency's activities. These will include: (1) the group whose dissatisfaction originally gave rise to the rule or law; (2) members of the policy-making body that approved it and who will ultimately be held responsible by their constituents for the costs and outcomes of the new policy; and (3) those organizations that find cause to relate, either cooperatively or competitively, with the implementing agency. For SEAs these vigilant groups include state legislatures, governors, Congress, federal agencies such as OE, school districts, educational interest groups, universities, educational materials suppliers, and private schools. To understand these relationships, it may be useful to view the dynamics of the implementation process in a systems perspective.

Inputs

Inputs are composed of *demands* and *resources*. Demands are the *raison d'être* for the system's development and for its continuing

FIGURE 4. A SYSTEMS PERSPECTIVE OF THE ROLE OF EXECUTIVE AGENCIES
IN THE POLICY-MAKING PROCESS

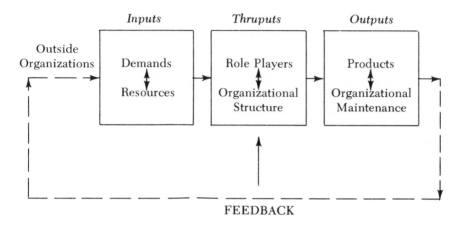

existence. That is, systems are designed to satisfy the needs of the society or specific elements of that society within which they exist. Organizations, a particular form of a system, are created and maintained to provide satisfaction for what are perceived to be important human needs. To satisfy demands, organizations attempt to produce sufficient human and material resources (e.g., money, space, equipment, and supplies). Material supports are required if the organization's human resources, those who will carry out relevant tasks, are to make the system operate.

SEAs have been formed and are maintained to oversee the implementation of educational programs that have been determined to be social needs according to state constitutions, legislatures, governors, and, more recently, Congress and OE. As perceived needs have increased, the states have provided greater support for widening definitions of minimum educational attainment. Once the states decided to play a role in the regulation and financing of education it was only a matter of time before SEAs were established and held responsible for assuring that policies approved by state governments would be implemented as intended. More recently, the expansion of the federal government's role in education, through 30 or more programs of categorical and other aid, requires that the SEAs, situated relatively equidistant between the federal government and the school districts, assure that the intent of these programs will be achieved. There is little doubt that the input of federal legislation has compounded the role requirements of the SEAs.

If the SEAs are to fulfill the expectations of policy makers at the state and the federal levels, adequate resources must be secured. Whether the resources made available are sufficient to meet increasing demands is difficult to ascertain, but it is clear that there has been a dramatic increase in resource inputs. The added human and material resources at the disposal of SEAs has been impressive, especially since the federal government has expanded its role in education. The Advisory Council on State Departments of Education concluded in 1969, that "although their responsibilities have swelled and their tasks have multiplied the *average* state education agency has only doubled its staff in the past 3 years."[2] Imagine the impact upon organizational life of *only* doubling staff in three years! Where are new staff members to be recruited from? Can sufficient numbers of qualified personnel be induced to join SEA staffs? How are they to be "socialized" into the existing organizational structure? These are questions we shall address.

Thruputs

Human and material resources must be patterned to facilitate the achievement of desired ends. That is, executive agencies charged with providing need satisfaction must organize resources in ways that support task accomplishment and put policy into practice. Leaders of these agencies have a dual responsibility. They have to assure that their organizations are so structured and staffed that they will be able to perform required tasks. At the same time they have to keep a close watch over external relations as they may be affected by new policy-implementation roles. These two complementary functions—*internal organization* for task performance and adjustment of *external relations* to meet changing conditions—constitute the core of thruput activities. The ability and willingness of SEAs to manage these functions determines the impact of intended policy and, in large measure, directly affects their own viability.

INTERNAL ORGANIZATION. To satisfy demands of policy makers SEA staff members perform a series of interrelated tasks that can be categorized as regulatory and developmental. SEAs monitor school districts' compliance with legislation and the intent of state constitutions. They are also responsible for seeing that the objectives of programs established by Congress and monitored by the OE and other federal agencies are pursued. Historically regulatory activities include accrediting school districts, auditing their expenditures, and certifying their professional staff. More recently SEAs have been required to approve program proposals and determine the outcomes of these programs. This has become especially relevant with the advent of federal aid because categorical aid programs frequently require evidence of compliance. SEAs have been charged with helping formulate programs and with devising and supervising evaluations of school district grant programs.

The SEAs, as the primary educational governance unit at the state level, can move beyond regulatory activity to perform developmental tasks that provide leadership for school systems in their states. The SEAs are the key linking organizations between policy-making bodies and the school districts that administer programs serving the demands of these bodies. There are many developmental tasks that SEAs can perform if they so desire. They can disseminate information by sponsoring regional conferences for school districts to explain the intent of educational programs legislated by Congress and the rules for obtaining funds under these programs. Similarly, many SEAs make information about successful educational practices available to school systems in their states. SEAs can also attempt to provide school districts with the skills of SEA personnel in such areas as curriculum development, supportive administrative services, computer programming, and educational media. As program responsibilities of school districts have grown these SEA personnel have increased, both in numbers and in diversity of competence.

Finally, SEAs can provide necessary guidance and set directions for public education. Recently SEAs have been pressured to establish needs and set long-range goals for education. As state and federal categorical aid programs have proliferated, long-range planning has become an urgent task. Such planning, in turn, calls for research concerning efficient and effective ways to attain educational goals. The role of SEAs in this respect is still somewhat unsettled because their limited manpower and expertise is in great demand for ongoing regulatory functions. Furthermore, universities,

the traditional centers of educational research, and the more recently established federally-sponsored research laboratories and development centers, dominate this activity.

To satisfy these growing expectations, SEA leaders must encourage staff relationships that facilitate task accomplishment. Figure 5 illustrates the interface or linking of people and structure to
manage required tasks.

The two factors that must be considered in staff management
are (1) the needs, role dispositions, and group affiliations of those
engaged to carry out tasks, and (2) the control, reward, and authority
structures devised to assure that members will perform adequately.
How the mix of these two factors develops varies from time to time
and place to place according to the objectives pursued and the dispositions of the organization's leaders. But both factors must be
present for policy to be implemented. Qualified people have to be
attracted to the organization and provided with structures that moti-
vate them to continue their efforts toward task accomplishment. Organizational leaders seek to establish conditions that foster task attainment based on recognition of the needs of organization
members. To do so they develop a formal hierarchy, encompassing
authority, control, and reward structures. Over time a system of
superior-subordinate relations with attendant rights and obligations
emerges to promote the effective functioning of interdependent organizational members.

EXTERNAL RELATIONS. Organizations must also seek to establish relatively predictable relationships with relevant external
bodies. As expectations for task attainment increase so will the number and complexity of external relations. There are three types of
organizations, or "organization-sets,"[3] that SEAs must deal with
effectively if they are to maintain their own preferred internal structure while implementing policy demands. These organizations can
be categorized as superior in authority, subordinate in authority,
and outside of the line of authority (see Figure 6).

Those organizations that are superior and subordinate to the
SEAs can be readily identified. Superior organizations include Congress, which passes laws, and OE, which establishes rules and regulations for the implementation of federal programs. At the state level
are the legislatures, which make laws and establish parameters for
the administration of state funded educational programs. Governors
see to their implementation and propose policies. The SEAs' function is to try to assure that the demands of these superior bodies are
satisfied.

FIGURE 5. INTRAORGANIZATIONAL THRUPUTS

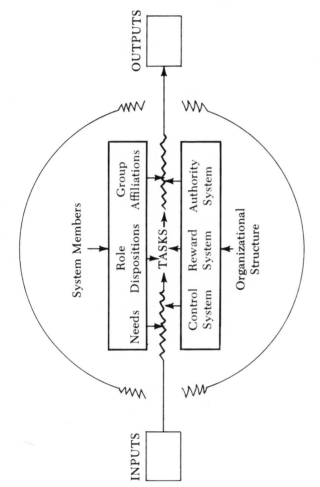

Source: Modified from Mike M. Milstein and James A. Beasco, eds., *Educational Administration and the Behavioral Sciences: A Systems Perspective* (Boston: Allyn & Bacon, 1973), p. 252; and Mike M. Milstein and Robert E. Jennings, *Educational Policy-Making and the State Legislature: The New York Experience* (New York: Praeger Publishers, 1973), p. 135.

FIGURE 6. EXTERNAL THRUPUTS: SEAS AND THEIR ORGANIZATION-SETS

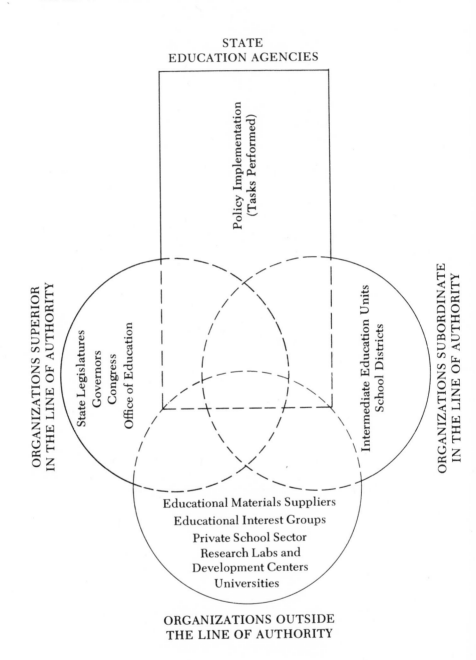

Subordinate organizations are the local school districts, which carry out program activities, and the mid-level education authorities, which in many states function as intermediate service units between SEAs and school districts. While these subordinate organizations are ultimately responsible to the state legislature for minimal educational attainment, in practice they receive communications from, and report directly to, the SEAs. As a result, SEAs have significant authoritative leverage over these intermediate and local educational organizations.

Organizations outside the line of authority present SEAs with a unique challenge because there are no rules and regulations for decision making when it comes to organizations not part of any overall authority structure. These organizations, including private schools, universities, research labs and development centers, educational interest groups, and educational materials suppliers, often have interests in common with SEAs, but there are no constraints that obligate them to coordinate their activities with SEAs.

The challenge to SEAs then is to reach out in rather undefined situations and develop interorganizational relationships. For example, educational materials suppliers provide textbooks and related products such as individualized instruction packages along with computer terminals and programmed instruction units for the schools. They often try to gear their products to meet the intent of the programs sponsored by states and the federal government. The SEAs, for their part, try to police this industry's activities to be sure that they comply with policy intent. But there are no legal requirements that the two cooperate or even keep each other informed. Similarly educational interest groups, representing teachers, administrators, school boards, and lay groups seek to shape the program thrusts of state and federal policy makers to meet local needs and, often, seek the cooperation of their SEAs in the effort. If cooperative relations can be established, SEAs can rely on these groups to encourage school districts' compliance with SEA policies. The extent to which such relationships are developed is heavily dependent upon the aggressiveness displayed by the agencies' leadership.

The SEAs are compelled to devise adequate ways of relating to external organizations or run the risk of being dominated by them, having their independence threatened, and possibly, losing the continued cooperation of vital personnel if they come to view the situation as intolerable. In adapting internally, the leaders of SEAs are able to turn to traditional bureaucratic mechanisms—reward, control, and authority. However these bureaucratic structures are not available when they seek to establish and maintain relations with outside organizations. Instead they have to devise extra-organizational, nonbureaucratic strategies of relating to assure that necessary resources are provided, agreed upon tasks are performed, and demands are held to a level that will not severely disrupt the organizational life of the agency.

The nonbureaucratic strategies employed by SEA leaders tend to vary across the several categories of organization-sets. For example it is unlikely that a strategy appropriate for dealing with school districts will be appropriate for dealing with interest groups. School districts can be subjected to the pressure of rules and regulations that accompany state and federal aid, but no such rules and regulations exist for dealing with interest groups.

Even differentiation by organization-sets is overly simplistic. School districts vary from one-room rural school houses to urban districts encompassing thousands of teachers and pupils. Logically, the expertise available to such diverse school systems and the influence they can wield with SEAs will vary. Thus SEAs must be highly sensitive to the strengths and weaknesses of each organization they work with if they expect to be effective in these relationships.

Inter-organizational behavior is significantly different in nature from intra-organizational behavior. Unfortunately, while there is much analysis of organizational behavior that focuses on relationships of subunits *within* organizations, there is little such analysis that focuses on relationships *between* organizations, particularly in education. The process by which organizations communicate with each other, make decisions and seek compliance when they cannot rely upon bureaucratic structures, is important but relatively unexplored. For this reason, and also because of the increasingly intergovernmental nature of educational policy making, how SEAs interact with environmental organizations is explored in some depth in Chapter IV.

Outputs

Organizations, as noted, try to satisfy needs by developing desired products. Products are difficult to define for educational organizations, and especially in the case of SEAs because these organizations are remote from the site of actual programs. SEAs can only support school districts as they attempt to satisfy demands of policy-making bodies for products in the form of students who have mastered a specified minimum knowledge base and/or who possess certain saleable skills. These product outputs can be roughly measured,* but they are indicators of school district success in achieving product outputs.

It could be argued that school districts are only able to produce desired outputs if SEAs satisfactorily provide required support in the form of consultation, planning, and evaluation. However, uncontrollable and potent variables, such as wealth of districts, parental support, and student attitudes, make this argument tenuous at best. Still, there are SEA products such as packaged curriculum guides, evaluation designs, and monitoring of resource inputs that can be judged for the impact they have on school districts. At another level, SEAs are held accountable for such long-range product outputs as needs assessments, goal setting, and the development and implementation of plans on predetermined time schedules. The demands made on the SEAs by the federal government during the 1960s and early 1970s provide opportunities to explore the success of SEAs in achieving these outputs. Federal programs such as the Elementary and Secondary Education Act require SEAs to perform assessment, planning, and evaluation functions. SEAs can choose to respond minimally to these requirements or to capitalize on the opportunities provided.

Aside from product outputs, complex organizations are concerned with another type of outcome: *organizational maintenance.* Maintenance outputs should cause those who participate in thruput activities to be relatively satisfied with results and be willing to continue to contribute to the effort. "Those who participate" refers to members of the organization and to members of organization-sets that provide resource inputs or carry out required tasks. There may be occasions when SEA leaders will have to forgo the development of or modify preferred product outputs in favor of maintaining good relationships with participants in the process. For example, it may be necessary for SEA officials to accept rather than challenge a state personnel board's ruling that new staff cannot be hired, even with federal funds. These leaders may conclude that they must reserve their limited influence for other and more important personnel de-

---

*For example, we can identify the number of pupils who pass an examination at the completion of a physics program, the level of reading achieved as a result of participation in an enriched reading-education program, the increases in intelligence-test achievement of students enrolled in preschool programs, or the percent of machine-shop graduates who are appropriately employed.

mands to be made in the future, and, therefore, they will probably defer and let the personnel board win this time around.

SEAs must be able to satisfy demands of policy-making bodies, organization-sets, and their own members. If they are unsuccessful in satisfying these demands, they will endanger the continued viability, or maintenance, of the organization. For example, if OE becomes unhappy about the lack of results of a federal education program administered by the SEAs, it can attempt to deal directly with school districts. Similarly, private schools may conclude that their cooperation with an SEA on a textbook distribution program has been unsatisfactory and appeal directly to the state legislature for required funds. Staff members of an SEA may feel that their work load, as a result of the increasing number of categorical programs established by the state legislatures or Congress, is unreasonable and resist efforts of their leaders to accomplish intended outcomes of such programs.

Feedback

The cycle of system activities is completed with feedback, which provides those making demands of and providing resources for the organization an opportunity to evaluate outputs against expectations. If they conclude that the outputs are inadequate or inappropriate they may choose to increase demands, (e.g., chastise or dismiss officials of the organization) or reduce, or even completely withdraw, future resource inputs. During the 1960s the California SEA found itself working under stress because a dissatisfied state legislature put severe constraints on its resource allocations. Of course, if efforts are viewed positively, support may increase as happened in Michigan where the SEA's campaign to establish needs assessments for the state was rewarded by official recognition and the passage of required legislation.

Because reception of outputs is so important, organizations attempt to obtain preliminary feedback and rectify apparent shortcomings before outputs are finalized. Thus SEA personnel may communicate through letters, by telephone, and by person-to-person contact with administrators at OE, with state legislators, or with the governor's lieutenants to appraise them of SEA activities and get their responses to these activities. This "early warning" system should indicate the reception their anticipated outputs will receive. The object is to modify undesired activities, or at least to change perceptions about them, and to emphasize activities that appear to be receiving favorable responses.

The Data Bases

The SEAs' responses to the impetus of two federal categorical aid programs—the National Defense Education Act of 1958 (NDEA) and the Elementary and Secondary Education Act of 1965 (ESEA) —are the focus of this study. The NDEA, enacted under the pressure of Soviet breakthroughs in space exploration, was intended to move the public schools toward emphasizing subjects that could meet the nation's preceived need for increased scientific capability. The ESEA, as noted in the act, was Congress' response to demands for the improvement of "educational quality and educational opportunities in the Nation's elementary and secondary schools," and in particular to provide educational enrichment programs for the "educationally deprived."[4] It was one of several responses to a felt need to break the vicious cycle of unending poverty that particularly afflicts the nation's minority groups. The several titles of these two acts specified program expectations that would, hopefully, facilitate need satisfaction. In both cases the SEAs have been allocated a major leadership and monitoring role.

How the SEAs have reacted to these federal inputs was explored over several years in three separate studies. The earliest exploration, two years after passage of the ESEA, was a single case study of the California SEA's administration of the NDEA and the ESEA.[5] The methods employed consisted of document analysis and interviews. Documents included legislative acts, rules and regulations, hearings and memoranda, tapes, external and internal evaluations of SEA, and school district performance, written records of state board meetings, staff minutes and other correspondences, as well as current relevant newspapers and journals. Interviews were conducted with SEA administrators, both those directly responsible for federal programs and top-level leaders of the organization; administrators in several California school districts; OE personnel who dealt with California SEA officials; congressional staff members; and leaders of organizations (interest group leaders, legislators, officers in other state agencies, university faculty) who had reason to work with California SEA personnel concerning these federal programs.

On the basis of the findings established in this study, a comparative case study was conducted in 1970.[6] This study entailed a return visit to the California SEA to observe whether activities had been modified over the more than three years since the earlier study. In addition, an analysis of responses to federal aid by the New York SEA was made and contrasted to that of the California SEA. Because of the difficulties involved in comparing the behavior of two complex SEAs, the analysis was limited to these SEAs' administration of ESEA titles. The California and New York SEAs were selected because of some important similarities and differences that might have explained variations in administrative behavior. They are similar in that they are the two largest SEAs in the nation, each serving the needs of large elementary and secondary enrollments, 4.6 million in California and 3.5 million in New York in 1970. They differ in relations with their respective state legislatures and governors and the methods of selection and powers of their chief state-school-officer and state boards of education. To assure relevant contrasts of the California SEA over time, the processes of analysis employed were the same as those used for the earlier study.

The final source of data comes from an 18-state survey conducted in 1971.[7] Based on the findings of the earlier studies, a survey instrument was designed to ascertain perceptions about the impact of the expanded federal role on the SEAs' ability to plan and carry out their assigned functions. The objective was to discover if the findings drawn in the earlier studies were generalizable. In addition it was hoped that the survey would provide answers to questions either not anticipated earlier or else not possible to answer in limited case studies. The surveyed states were selected to include SEAs varying in geographical regions, number of personnel, and selection process for SEA chief officers. Respondents included Washington-based OE administrators who played specific roles in working with SEAs, school district administrators, SEA administrators of NDEA and ESEA titles, chief SEA officers and their immediate assistants, and educational administration professors. Fifty-three percent of the 370 officials surveyed responded at the time of the analysis. (See Figure 7.)

An effort has also been made to contrast and compare the findings of these studies with the few similar studies of SEAs conducted by other researchers. In particular the reader will find frequent reference to the Berke and Kirst team's analysis of the response of six SEAs to federal aid and Murphy's analysis of ESEA Title I and ESEA Title V as it was implemented by the SEAs.[8]

FIGURE 7.   TYPOLOGY OF THE STATES INCLUDED IN THE SURVEY

	SEA Personnel* (Fiscal Year 1970)			Geographical Location				Superintendent	
	250 or less	250 to 500	500 or more	South	East	Mid-West	West	Elected	Appointed
Alabama		348.8		X				X	
Arizona	142.1						X	X	
Colorado	203.2						X		X
Connecticut		463.8			X				X
Florida			846.0	X				X	
Georgia			874.3	X				X	
Idaho	97.0						X	X	
Illinois			840.0			X		X	
Indiana		265.0				X		X	
Minnesota		374.0				X			X
Nebraska	160.0					X			X
New Jersey			674.0		X				X
Ohio			590.0			X			X
Oregon	208.5						X	X	
Rhode Island	249.0				X				X
South Carolina		448.0		X				X	
Tennessee		426.0		X				X	
Texas			831.0	X					X

*SEA personnel data abstracted from U.S. Department of Health, Education, and Welfare, Office of Education, *State Departments of Education and Federal Programs.* (Washington, D.C.: U.S. Government Printing Office, 1972), Table 4, pp. 10-11.

The major ferment in changing federal-state relations was at its zenith during the time period covered by the field work and the efforts of other analysts. Much of what has followed in federal-state interactions has been an effort to consolidate and regularize the relationships forged during that period. This conclusion is also shared by Berke and Kirst and the members of their research team.[9]

The systems framework has been extremely helpful in organizing the findings of these several explorations into SEA responses to federal categorical aid programs. Chapter I considers the *inputs* provided for education at the state and federal levels and details how these inputs have been translated into demands and resources for SEAs. Chapters III and IV focus on *thruputs* as personnel and organizational structure are brought together to process demands and resources to attain desired outcomes. Chapter V focuses on a complementary thruput activity, how SEAs relate with organizations that are superior and subordinate in the authority structure, as well as how they relate with organizations outside of the authority structure. Chapter VI considers, in closing, the impact of federal aid on SEAs, their responses, and the *outputs* or results of their efforts, and offers suggestions regarding modifications in the process that might help SEAs more fully meet expectations.

III / Internal Activities: Regulatory and Developmental Tasks

Organizations are established and maintained to satisfy needs. In the case of the SEAs, needs that were initially outlined by state constitutions and later specified by state legislatures and governors have been expanded as a result of federal initiatives. Federal funds, in the form of categorical aid programs, are flowing into and through the SEAs in unprecedented amounts. The possibilities and problems confronting the SEAs as a result of this input are also unprecedented. The response options open to these agencies depend in part upon idiosyncrasies that exist in each state, in the magnitude of their educational needs, the values and administrative styles of SEA leaders, and the relationship between an SEA and its state legislature and governor's office. Yet there are overall patterns evolving that can be identified to help us establish a better understanding of the process of change in these complex organizations.

In this chapter the focus is on responses devised by SEAs to incorporate the NDEA and the ESEA into their organizational structures. The presentation is based on the dynamics of the policy implementation process introduced in Chapter II. Specifically, we will explore the impact that administrative requirements of the NDEA and the ESEA have had on internal thruput tasks performed by SEAs. These tasks, which will be categorized as *regulatory* and *developmental,* serve a single purpose: they enable the SEAs to enforce "laws and rules and regulations that require local school districts to meet particular standards and comply with specific conditions."[1]

How SEAs manage their tasks is highly dependent on two factors. The first factor is their human resources: the SEA staff's ability to accomplish their assigned tasks. Personnel are required in growing numbers, but quantity of staff is not the only concern. The SEAs' recruitment process and in-service training efforts affect the kind of personnel brought together and their subsequent effectiveness. The second factor is their organizational structures: the NDEA and the ESEA have expanded and multiplied the responsibilities of SEAs and these responsibilities must be integrated and coordinated.

Tasks Differentiated

It is useful to divide SEA tasks into regulatory and developmental. Regulatory tasks, which are specific manifestations of the SEAs' responsibility to seek compliance by school districts with laws, rules, regulations, and guidelines, can be viewed as the outcome or institutionalization of demands for change. They are backward looking in that they are performed to assure that policies already developed are implemented. They are *reactive* in nature, putting into practice that which has survived the policy-making process.

Developmental tasks are usually non-mandatory and are carried out by SEAs when they seek to play a role that goes beyond the mere policing of school district activities. SEAs are required to provide minimal regulatory supervision but only those SEAs with sufficient inclination and capability will move beyond this level to provide support and leadership for their states' school districts. Developmental tasks, in contrast to regulatory tasks, can thrust SEAs into a *proactive* stance, involving them in the formative stages of the policy-making process. If they pursue developmental activities such as generating information, clarifying goals, setting priorities, and recommending program preferences to policy makers, SEAs can influence debates about policy options before decisions are made.

Regulatory Tasks

Regulation attempts to insure that school districts comply with particular conditions set by policy makers, whether at the state or federal level. What compliance means and how it is to be assured has usually been left to the interpretation of SEA officials. In the California SEA, as an example, preliminary discussion about the NDEA revolved around what the state's responsibilities would be and which division should administer the program. One internal faction argued that the NDEA was an equipment-distribution program and, as such, the SEA's only responsibility would be to assure that school district records of equipment purchased and dollars spent be checked for accuracy. Therefore, they reasoned, the NDEA program should become the responsibility of the Division of Public School Administration, which functioned as a monitoring unit for school district activities in noninstructional areas such as textbook acquisition, school lunch programs, and buildings and facilities. This suggestion was countered by another faction arguing that the NDEA was meant to serve specific educational objectives and therefore should be administered by the Division of Instruction, which it eventually was.

The point of the example is that SEAs, depending upon how they interpret federal programs, can respond minimally, limiting their role to the preparation and submission of brief accounting and evaluation reports to OE; or respond more broadly, encouraging school districts to operate efficient and effective educational programs. To illustrate this two SEA regulatory activities, school district audits and evaluation, will be examined.

Audits

Accounting for school district purchases and expenditures was an SEA regulatory task long before the NDEA and the ESEA were passed and thus this basic enforcement task has not presented them with a significant problem. For the main part, it has only required that SEAs extend the manpower available for this effort. However, most SEAs have been reluctant to assign professionals to auditing tasks.[2] The advent of federal programs has compounded the need for SEAs to provide expert consultant help in subject matter areas for school districts. Therefore, when limited resources require that a choice be made between an auditor or a consultant, the latter normally takes precedence.

Even more important is the SEAs' traditional reliance on the ability and honesty of school district administrators. This is due in part to their tendency to treat each other with professional deference,[3] but it is also related to their need to maintain the continuing good will of school district administrators. Without them SEAs could not meet their auditing responsibilities unless they drastically increased the number of personnel committed to this task. School district administrators relieve SEAs of auditing efforts by providing complete sets of accounting records. Given these realities, SEAs are not inclined to audit district expenditures too critically: the backlash from a more aggressive auditing stance may be the withdrawal of local cooperation on which the limited SEA staff must largely depend. It is not surprising that many state-level administrators disparage the "red tape" associated with federal programs; in part they are reflecting and representing their constituencies in the school districts.

Evaluation

SEA evaluation of school district programs is highly dependent upon external expectations, perhaps more so than any other tasks they perform. In 1958, when the NDEA was passed, there was little demand for identified local outcomes from federal aid, but by 1965, when the ESEA was passed, the situation had changed markedly. The contrast in SEA evaluation efforts regarding the NDEA and the ESEA is understandable only if one considers the shifts in external expectations that occurred between passage of the two acts. In the seven-year interim period the costs of formal education had soared and it became clear that large urban school systems were unable to meet the challenges presented by school populations shifting rapidly in composition from white and middle class to minority and lower class.

Largely as a result of these two realities the great debate over national assessment began in earnest. Furthermore, accountability practices, such as Program, Planning, Budgeting Systems (PPBS) advocated by national leaders like former Secretary of Defense Robert McNamara, were taking hold in government, particularly at the federal level. Such practices were bound to increase the pressure to evaluate outcomes of federal education programs.

In the enabling legislation of the NDEA, evaluation was most noticeable by its absence. The only statement related to evaluation (Section 1004) required the SEAs to "make such reports to the Commissioner, in such form and containing such information as may be reasonably necessary to enable the Commissioner to perform his duties." Regulations pursuant to the act gave at least minimal attention to this need by requiring provision "for periodic evaluation by the State agency of the programs and their administration."[4] However, no specificity was given to the meaning of "periodic evaluation" and OE did not issue its first formal set of NDEA guidelines until September 1963, five years after the NDEA became law. Furthermore, evaluation as such was not addressed until the guidelines were revised in 1965. Even at this late date OE went no further than to remind SEAs that "A State should be guided by the question, Has instruction been improved and strengthened?"[5]

Left adrift without prior experience or clear directives from the federal level, it is not surprising that the SEAs' record of evaluation for NDEA programs is not impressive. Of California's 11-point scheme used to select projects for funding, only one is concerned with evaluation of the projects effectiveness. Assuming that applying school districts make strong presentations on the other ten points, it is highly unlikely that their grant requests will be turned down for lack of a viable evaluation scheme.

By 1965 the call for accountability in education had surfaced. As a result, policy makers demanded proof of attainment in ESEA programs, especially those funded through ESEA Title I. SEAs were required to approve *only* those program applications that contained

> objective measurement of educational achievement . . . in meeting the special educational needs of educationally deprived children . . . including information relating to the educational achievement of students participating in programs carried out under this title . . . [School districts] will keep such records . . . as the State educational agency may find necessary to assure the correctness and verification of such reports.[6]

The language of this act and its subsequent regulations and guidelines regarding evaluation is much more specific than that of the NDEA. However, demand is one thing; compliance is quite another. After reviewing the results of the first year of ESEA Title I, OE officials concluded that evaluation efforts had fallen far short of expectations. In general, "the returns were not of sufficient quality to make an accurate evaluation of the effectiveness of Title I programs."[7] Their report concluded that the most conspicuous problems for many SEAs were to secure personnel (38 states) and to establish evaluation techniques (37 states). These problems still plague SEAs.

Lack of qualified evaluation personnel and the slow development of evaluation techniques in SEAs are partially the result of organizational hiring practices. Staff recruited by SEAs tend to come from the ranks of schoolpeople, who often are not prepared as evaluators. Given their own recent backgrounds at the local level, they are not inclined toward the application of stringent, state-level performance standards. Because most SEA administrators want to maintain good relations with the school districts they are charged with evaluating, they tend to resist making vigorous demands on school personnel responsible for establishing outcomes of their districts' federal programs. As a result, SEA officials often defer to the judgments of school staff when it comes to evaluation and rarely question program results extensively. In the words of an SEA official in New York charged with evaluation, "the districts know what evaluation means and they do a good job." But even when they assume that district-level officials are unprepared for the task, SEA personnel are often patient. Iannaccone concludes that in Massachusetts "state officials feel that it will take time for local school systems to become accustomed to and capable of doing and using evaluations; and until that time the state should not interfere."[8]

To compound the problem, in many SEAs where evaluation units had already been established, federal-program evaluations have been added to their work load. Not required in the past to carry out sophisticated evaluation efforts, personnel in these units resist efforts to update their skills or pressure school district officials to upgrade their evaluation capabilities. Furthermore, where all evaluation personnel are housed in a single unit, it is not likely that specific program needs will be as fully monitored as they will be where evaluation personnel are housed in units that concentrate on single federal programs.

The Office of Compensatory Education in the California SEA is an example of the concentrated approach. The Title I evaluation team is housed *within* a program-specific office, not in a task-specific centralized evaluation unit. The core office staff perceived that federal and state policy-makers emphasized evaluation, so they set up a special unit for it, and committed six professional positions to fill. From the start, the office's planning group felt that the SEA's central evaluation unit, the Bureau of Educational Research, could not possibly manage ESEA Title I evaluation tasks because it had no desire to "get tough" with school districts. Furthermore, they felt that evaluation would be retarded if placed with this unit because it had only four staff members and the state legislature, which was dissatisfied with the effectiveness of the SEA, would refuse to increase the unit's staff to the extent that the ESEA I evaluation effort required. The planning group concluded that the unique evaluation techniques called for could only be developed in a unit committed *solely* to the ESEA Title I program and staffed by persons chosen on the basis of their proven evaluation skills, not on the basis of their affinity to, or relations with, schoolpeople whose programs they would have to evaluate.

The subsequent effort and the dedication and skill of the staff members responsible for ESEA Title I evaluation in California had much to do with both the praise the Office of Compensatory Education has enjoyed and the criticism it has had to bear. The California ESEA I evaluation effort has been noted by OE officials as one of the best in the country.[9] This conclusion has been shared grudgingly by school district officials in California who have had to comply with the office's demands. On occasion more than a few have felt the need to complain to their state legislators or congressmen about the severity of the office's evaluation demands.

Such evaluations are still the exception rather than the rule. There are calls for improved efforts: "Evaluative techniques will need to be employed in order to improve the decision-making process in education" notes Commissioner Nyquist of the New York SEA,[10] but there are few indications that SEAs are prepared to meet this need. Furthermore, there is little indication that the federal government will provide the support required to improve evaluation even if the SEAs become more concerned and upgrade their ability to do so. As Murphy has noted, "Since the beginning of the program, evaluation has been high on the list of federal rhetorical priorities, but low on the list of actual USOE priorities. The reasons for this are many. They include fear of upsetting the federal-state balance, recognition . . . that little expertise exists at the state and local level to evaluate a broad-scale reform program, and fear of disclosing failure. No administrator is anxious to show that his program is not working."[11]

But the lack of federal support is probably due mostly to the fact that educational decision-making cannot be separated from political decision-making. In October 1965 Francis Keppel, then U.S. Commissioner of Education, attempted to withhold ESEA Title I funds from the Chicago school district, claiming, among other things, that audits of that district's books indicated inappropriate expenditures of previous Title I funds. As might be expected, enormous pressure was put on Illinois's congressmen by officials of the Chicago school district. They, in turn, put pressure on the executive branch and Keppel was forced to retract his order and issue approval for release of the funds. The lesson was not lost on state and local governmental officials, as Murphy noted: "While congressmen abhor waste and never tire of abusing bureaucrats who countenance waste, these are general principles which do not necessarily apply to individual cases, particularly if alleged misuses occur in their own districts."[12] OE officials have concluded that there are severe limits on their ability to provide substantial support for SEAs that challenge school districts to meet the letter of the law.

In conclusion, most SEAs, as a result of federal aid, do more regulating than they did prior to the initiation of aid programs but still do only as much as is required of them. This is due in part to manpower shortages, but it also appears to be related to professional norms of SEA and school-district officials, and to the inability of OE to hold the line against political pressure from these officials and their friends in Congress.

Developmental Tasks

There is some feeling that SEAs should set educational priorities in their states. Whether they will be able to do so is still questionable, although a recent OE report indicates that SEAs are moving in this direction: "A considerable number of State departments of education have in the past few years undergone changes in their basic orientation. In general, departments have moved away from heavy regulatory responsibilities . . . more time is being allotted to increased leadership responsibilities . . ."[13] But there are others who feel that SEAs are still trapped in their regulatory chores.

SEAs have an initial advantage if they choose to play a proactive role. As the designated state administrative agencies charged with overseeing educational activities they are at the center of the three-tiered federal system and they can normally count on a steady flow of information from above (OE) and from below (school districts). They are in a logical position to synthesize this information and set fundamental directions. But to do so they must initiate comprehensive planning, identify educational needs, and devise means to attenuate these needs. To ascertain the SEAs' responses to the challenge we will focus first on their planning activities and then turn to the efforts they have made to establish statewide and departmental goals.

SEA Planning

Current planning efforts of SEAs should be placed in the context of their organizational history. Until the 1960s most SEAs were relatively small agencies; the planning abilities of their few staff members were somewhat limited. In addition their responsibilities were narrowly defined as largely regulatory. As the states began to shoulder more responsibility for education, the need for an improved SEA planning capacity became increasingly apparent.

Federal categorical education programs channeled through the SEAs since the 1960s have compounded the need for SEA planning. At the same time the fiscal resources made available for SEA staff development have improved their potential to become more effective planning agencies. The SEA response to the challenge to plan is still in the developmental stage, but it is possible to assess evolving patterns as they consolidate this flurry of activity.

SEA planning capabilities are perceived as rather poor. Even many SEA personnel view their planning as somewhat chaotic. One top-level administrator in California confided that his SEA "hasn't done much short-range planning, let alone long-range planning." SEA staff have a sense of frustration because much time is reserved for planning but little seems to result from it. One respondent of the 18-state survey, an SEA official from Texas, found himself in a rather typical dilemma; he had to "carry out a regularly assigned job plus serve on numerous task forces and continuing committees . . . [that] meet so often that few meetings have over 50% attendance." This response was similar to that of an SEA administrator from Georgia who felt that there should be "less planning for planning's sake and more planning to mobilize the SEA to direct its efforts toward effective program administration." In short while SEAs are often viewed as making efforts to plan, the results of these efforts appear minimal, even to those who participate in SEA planning efforts.

There are several SEA characteristics that help explain unenthusiastic assessments of SEA planning effectiveness. First, and probably most important, is the fact that planning appears to take place at the lower organizational levels much more frequently than at the top levels of the SEAs. Respondents to the survey were asked at which SEA level most planning took place. The information obtained is summarized in Figure 8.

Not a single group of respondents thought that much planning occurs at the top SEA level. On the contrary, three of the four groups saw this level as the place where planning occurs *least* frequently. Equally important, three of the groups, most notably SEA and OE administrators who should have reason to know, felt that the individual program level is the place where planning is *most* frequently

FIGURE 8.   WHERE PLANNING ACTIVITY IS CARRIED ON IN THE SEAs*

GROUPS	Superintendent's Office Planning Most/Least	Division Level Planning Most/Least	Bureau Level Planning Most/Least	Individual Program Level Planning Most/Least
SEA Administrators N=102	X			X
OE Administrators N=8	X			X
School District Administrators N=36	X	X		
Professors of Educational Administration N=38			X	X

*For purposes of the survey *division* was defined as higher in the organizational level than *bureau*. "No responses" are not included; these ranged from a high of 67% "no responses" for school-district personnel to a low of 13% "no responses" for OE personnel.
   Source: Mike M. Milstein, "Federally Funded Educational Programs and State Education Agencies" (Report to Improving State Leadership in Education, Denver, 1970), p. 6.

carried on. Thus planning is an activity associated with the lowest rather than the highest levels of the SEA structure.

   One OE administrator concluded that "nobody minds the store" when it comes to planning in SEAs. This awareness and concern is shared at the state level. An SEA administrator from Idaho felt that it is vital to have "a clear commitment to planning communicated from top administration." Similarly, a top-level planner for the New York SEA commented that "unless planning is to be an exercise in completing blank forms whose fate becomes a long shelf line, key decision-makers must have the time necessary to plan."[14] In short, before planning can be effective there will have to be a change in attitudes, skills, and priorities among top-level SEA administrators. Without top-level involvement it is unlikely that

FIGURE 9. PLANNING EFFORTS RELATED TO SIZE OF SEA

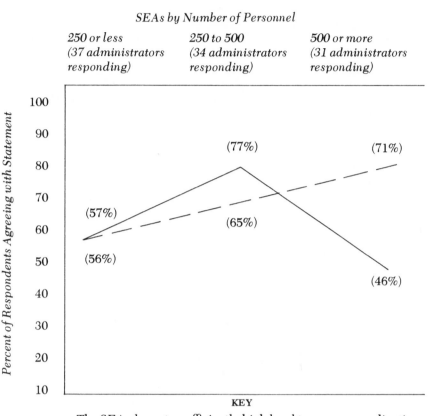

SEAs by Number of Personnel

250 or less	*250 to 500*	*500 or more*
(37 administrators	*(34 administrators*	*(31 administrators*
responding)	*responding)*	*responding)*

KEY
——— The SEA plans at a sufficiently high level to assure co-ordination.
– – – The SEA does a good job of assessing educational needs.

planning efforts will lead to comprehensive, long-range direction-setting for the states' educational efforts.

A second SEA characteristic that influences planning is the size of agency staffs. When SEAs represented in the survey were subdivided according to staff size (less than 250, 250 to 500, and more than 500 personnel) administrators from the middle group viewed their agencies as doing the best job of co-ordinating planning activities. Administrators from the largest group perceived their agencies as most competent at assessing educational needs. (See Figure 9.)

FIGURE 10.   SEA PLANNING ACTIVITIES: PERCEPTIONS OF SEA ADMINIS-
TRATORS WITH ELECTED AND APPOINTED STATE SUPERINTENDENTS*

Item	SEA Administrators Where Chief School Officer is Elected (N=52)		SEA Administrators Where Chief School Officer is Appointed (N=50)	
	%Agree	%Disagree	%Agree	%Disagree
Comprehensive planning is carried on by the SEA:	60	41	48	52
The SEA has done a good job of assessing educational needs in the state:	80	20	46	54
The SEA has set clear priorities concerning educational objectives to be pursued:	57	43	32	68

*Percentages may not always equal 100% due to rounding.

These responses indicate that differences in SEA planning abilities may be explained, at least partially, on the basis of size. It may be that co-ordination is most feasible when an SEA is large enough to employ specialists yet small enough to retain a sense of overall organizational identity. However, when major long-range planning activities such as statewide assessments are required, it may be that only large SEAs have an adequate base of personnel and the fiscal resources to do a sufficient job.

Another SEA characteristic that appears related to planning is the process by which the state's chief school official is selected. In 1972 these chief officials were selected as follows: 27 were appointed by state boards of education, 19 were elected by popular vote, and four were appointed by governors.[15] The survey responses were categorized according to whether the chief official was elected or appointed, which led to some interesting resultant distinctions, as indicated in Figure 10. Respondent groups from states where the chief official is elected were more positive about their SEAs' comprehensive planning, assessment of educational needs, and priority setting than were respondents from states where he is appointed. Most interesting, SEA administrators from states with an elected school head were consistently more positive about their SEAs' planning activities than were their counterparts from states with an appointed school head.

Educators have long contended that selections for key educational posts such as chief SEA administrator should be based on recommendations from the profession to assure that educationally sound programs are pursued and to avoid political manipulation of the education system. Yet respondents from states where the chief administrator is elected were more favorably impressed with their SEAs' planning efforts than were those from states where he is appointed. In the final analysis the political relationships of the elected superintendent may be an important asset. He may be able to use his popular support to apply leverage in dealing with the legislature, the governor, and interest groups, thus maintaining a wide latitude for SEA planning discretion.

IMPORTANCE OF FEDERAL AID. Given the generally unenthusiastic views expressed by survey respondents regarding SEA planning performance, especially by those from within SEAs, the question is whether the situation is being improved or further complicated as a result of federal involvement. The answer, it would seem, is that federal intervention is a positive factor; at least most survey respondents—93% of the SEA administrators, 88% of the OE administrators, 97% of the school district administrators, and 79% of the professors of educational administration—felt that the federal impact has improved SEA planning.

The importance of federal programs for SEA planning depends in large part on the resources available to SEAs. These resources, which vary from program to program, can be viewed at two levels. First, there are those provided for administration, such as ESEA Title I resources. The quantity of dollars made available for the administration of this program has provided the flexibility required for enterprising SEA recruiters to hire personnel who view planning as a legitimate administrative activity. Such large resource inputs, even though targeted for administrative purposes, enable the SEAs, if they so choose, to pursue developmental tasks such as planning. The bigger SEAs have an additional advantage in that their administrative support, an amount equaling one percent of the total Title I school district allocation, is quite large. For example, during fiscal year 1969, California and New York received $802,900 and $1,204,000 respectively to support administrative chores related to ESEA Title I.[16]

However, many SEA administrators would argue that regulatory chores associated with federal and state programs are so demanding that there really are not sufficient resources available for planning, even with inputs such as provided through ESEA Title I. As summed up by an SEA administrator from Colorado, they feel that SEAs need "risk capital or non-obligatory money which can be used to build a planning capability." In this regard Bailey and Mosher found that 13 of the 32 state school heads who responded to their inquiry about the impact of the ESEA on SEAs identified the inadequacy of funds for planning as a "particular hardship."[17]

In response to this criticism Congress has included resources for SEA *planning* in grants such as ESEA Titles III and V. Title III authorizes grants to states for establishing supplementary educational centers to provide services not otherwise available in sufficient quantity and quality. More specifically, according to the enabling legislation, the purpose of Title III is "to stimulate and assist in the development and establishment of exemplary elementary and secondary school educational programs to serve as models for regular school programs." Before 1968 OE directly approved school district proposals, a responsibility that was then shifted to the state level. Whether the SEAs can capitalize on this shift in resources and responsibilities is still uncertain. The SEAs in the two super-states represent contrasting responses. California's SEA became concerned about planning in the early 1960s, before most SEAs,[18] but it has since been severely constrained by the state legislature, which has interfered with ESEA Title III decision-making by mandating program priorities and administrative procedures for achieving these priorities. The New York SEA, in contrast, has been able to remain free of such political entanglements and has developed a highly respected Title III unit, the Center for Planning and Innovation. This unit has been instrumental in the SEA's gradual move toward comprehensive planning, both for internal organizational functioning and for statewide educational direction-setting.

ESEA Title V, Section 503, is the one federal program that is specifically aimed at expanding and upgrading SEA planning activities. Title V can be viewed as the outcome of the federal government's concern that SEAs may not plan sufficiently to achieve the intent of the other titles of the act. Its resources may be used to advance statewide educational planning; improve data collection, storage, and retrieval; disseminate information about educational programs; conduct or sponsor research; publish and distribute curricular materials; improve teacher preparation programs; measure statewide student achievement; train SEA or school-district personnel; and provide school districts with consultative and technical services on educational matters.

Because the range of acceptable projects is very broad, it is quite difficult for OE to closely monitor SEA Title V activities. As a result, the quality of ESEA Title V projects is almost totally dependent on actions taken within the SEAs. If SEAs take the initiative it would seem that Title V, of all the federal programs, could most directly enhance their comprehensive planning capacity. Unfortunately, as Murphy concludes, this stimulus has not had its intended effects. "Title V resulted in SEA staff and budget growth, but expansion took place largely in traditional areas."[19] "Title V decisions did not grow out of the sequential process of assessing needs, establishing overall objectives, analyzing various alternatives, and then making a choice. SEAs neither defined 'strengthening' nor established general priorities before deciding on specific projects."[20] It should be noted that Murphy doubts that SEAs could have done more. He develops the idea that *all* organizations possess attributes that mitigate against searching for "best" solutions. He believes that organizations focus on "short-term problems" instead of "developing long-term strategies."[21]

Most SEAs have not set priorities for subunit requests for ESEA Title V funding. In part this is because Title V coordinators rarely have authority to control Title V expenditures by others who are higher in the bureaucratic pecking order. Given this reality it would be surprising if comprehensive planning was improved as a result of the injection of Title V resources.

From fiscal year 1966 through fiscal year 1970 the SEAs' expenditures of Title V funds were categorized by OE as noted in Figure 11. The portion of Title V dollars reserved for comprehensive planning by SEAs during those years has been noticeably low. Furthermore, it decreased from almost 25% in 1966 to just under 16% in 1970. It is also interesting that services for local school districts (the third and fourth categories) command a large and growing portion of Title V resources (24% in 1966 and up to 47% in 1970).

CONSTRAINTS OF FEDERAL AID. SEA officials are quick to note that their planning inadequacies are compounded by the constraints that accompany federal aid. In particular they criticize (1)

FIGURE 11.   PERCENT OF ESEA TITLE V (SECTION 503) GRANTS SPENT BY
SEAs IN MAJOR FUNCTION CATEGORIES FOR FISCAL YEARS 1966-70

Categories	1966	1967	1968	1969	1970
General administration	44	38	33	36	28
Program planning, development, and evaluation	25	22	19	17	16
Services for improvement of instruction in school districts	19	23	34	32	34
Services for improvement of administration in school districts	5	8	7	5	13
Accreditation, licensing, and staff development	5	6	5	8	7
Services for agency-operated institutions and programs and "other"	2	3	2	2	2

Source: U.S. Department of Health, Education, and Welfare, Office of Education, *State Departments of Education and Federal Programs* (Washington, D.C., U.S. Government Printing Office, 1972), p. 5. The original data have been modified by combining the "agency-operated" and "other" categories and by rounding off numbers to the nearest percent.

the way federal programs are packaged, (2) the lack of lead time prior to the initiation of programs, (3) the tardiness of actual release of federal funds, and (4) the tenuous nature of the federal allocation process.

Regarding the *packaging of programs,* federal aid can come to the states in the form of categorical aid programs, which specify outcome expectations according to particular groups of students, or it can come as general aid programs that leave discretion for the establishment of program objectives and program management to the states. General aid can also be distributed without specification of functional areas such as education, welfare, or highways. Such aid leaves state policy-makers with *total* discretion for distribution of resources. There is some argument as to which of these forms of aid most facilitates SEA planning.

The preferences of survey respondents reflect and highlight the conflict that has long existed between federal- and state-level educators. OE administrators responding to the survey unanimously share Congress' view that programs must be kept highly specific to assure that SEAs and school districts plan for and achieve national policies. At the state level, responding SEA administrators and school district officials clearly prefer general federal aid by functional areas with "no strings" attached to resource transfers. They argue that the problems and abilities of states differ markedly and that they are in the best position to decide *what* needs to be done and *how* it should be done. As one SEA administrator from Florida noted, "highly categorical federal programs, by their very nature, discourage planning at the state level since fewer options are open for consideration."

This point of view appears sound until tested against reality. ESEA Title V comes closer than all other federal aid programs to the preferences of state-level administrators. Other than generally encouraging planning, it does not specify intended outcomes or program administration so there is much latitude for state-level choices as to the tasks to be achieved. However, there is little evidence that SEAs have employed Title V dollars to plan, establish priorities, or set goals. This is not to conclude that the federal view is more appropriate. Severely restrictive categorical aid programs may assure that SEAs do not stray far from intended program outcomes, but they do little to encourage SEAs to plan, which would seem to be a prerequisite for more effective deployment of state and federal resources.

A second issue is the lack of *lead time* to establish activities before a federal program becomes operational. Congress normally does not move proposed or amended programs through committees, to the floor and across chambers for approval until well into the legislative session. As a result educational programs are frequently authorized only a few months before they are actually launched. Program initiation for SEAs and school districts usually requires more time than this process permits. Inevitably, a crisis environment dominates state and local activities during the start-up period of new or amended federal aid programs that are not announced until just before the academic year begins. Patterns of response developed to cope with such pressures can easily become habit-forming for SEAs, making it difficult for them to evolve more comprehensive organizational planning responses. At one and the same time they have to select staff, develop organizational structures, find housing, "get the word out" to the field, and establish rules, regulations and proposal-selection criteria. Comprehensive planning is virtually impossible in such a situation.

In the long run it may be to the advantage of SEAs and school districts to decline to participate in federal programs that are initiated on short notice if the result is dislocation rather than enrichment of their educational programs. However, this is difficult to do politically; it is not easy to explain to policy makers, be they school board members or state legislators, that a state or school district should not accept external funds when internal resources are scarce.

Late funding can also be a problem. Federal programs are susceptible to procedural difficulties that can result in funds being delayed even into the year when programs are supposed to be operating. Frequently school districts are forced to find local dollars to initiate programs or else delay their start while they wait for Congress, the Office of Management and Budget, OE, and their SEA to filter allocation to the district level. Congress' activities are based on the calendar year (January 1 to December 31) while the activities of school districts are based on the academic year (July 1 to June 30) so overlaps and gaps in funding authorization tend to occur.* After Congress finally authorizes and appropriates funds, expenditures must be allocated by the President, cleared by the Office of Management and Budget, and dispersed by OE to the SEAs and school districts. It is not unusual that grants reach school districts when programs are already more than half over.

A good example of the extensive delay in funding occurred for fiscal year 1967 when Congress did not decide upon final appropriations until October 1966; the Bureau of the Budget (the predecessor to the Office of Management and Budget) withheld funds until December of that year; OE did not complete its computation of entitlements until the end of February 1967. In fact, exact entitlements did not actually reach the school districts until the middle of March 1967. As a result, knowledge of exact grants did not come to school districts until many of their programs were almost completed.

Finally, long-range planning regarding federal programs is

---

*When asked whether Congress will modify its practices to assure that federal funds reach school districts before programs are due to start, one high-level OE administrator responded: "in view of the fact that all education programs have been operating under continuing resolutions, with funds doled out quarter by quarter or month by month, this sounds grimly humorous!"

complicated by the *tenuous nature of the federal allocation process,* including numerous program amendments, formula distribution changes, and allocations that tend to revolve upward and downward annually. Nothing is certain in the year-to-year funding of federal programs. Tasks usually increase when SEAs become committed to planning activities so there is justifiable concern at the state level that the continuous flow of required federal resources cannot be relied upon. For example, 1970 ESEA Title V grants—due to a combination of changes in the formula, the addition of portions of NDEA Title III, and inflation—were actually down by 20% from the 1967 Title V grants. Such uncertainties also affect other programs. In New York the ESEA Title II director was forced to drop a five-year survey after only three years because federal funds allocated to her unit were severely reduced.

The problem is of such magnitude that some SEA officials recommend that SEAs should not accept a role in managing federal programs unless there is a hard commitment in the form of funds attached to enable the SEAs to get on with required planning. An alternative might be to borrow state funds for planning and return them to state treasuries when federal funds arrive. However, most state governors and legislatures are sufficiently wary of federal funding procedures to resist such requests from state agencies.

When SEA administrators decry federal constraints on planning there are noticeably few complaints about OE officials. Generally, state-level administrators view their federal counterparts as doing their best to be helpful. Whether this perception is due to a realistic estimate of OE performance or to the mutual expectations of professionals who perform complementary tasks at different governmental levels, the potential for useful OE inputs into SEA planning is probably great. Of the SEA administrators who responded to the federal-impact survey, 89% felt that federal guidelines are highly useful and 81% felt that OE personnel are important human resources that SEAs can employ as they get on with planning activities. A majority (63%) felt that OE's State Management Review service, which has been offered since 1969 to the SEAs in conjunction with ESEA Title V, is helpful in their efforts to plan. A voluntary program, it is intended to help SEAs strengthen their administration of federal and state programs. OE personnel work in cooperation with SEA officials who are invited to analyze their own planning, project administration, evaluation, information dissemination, personnel and fiscal management, and general administration and organization.[22] Because data are self-generated by SEA officials there has been some criticism as to the value of these efforts for improving SEA administrative performance.

In summary, SEA administrators give satisfactory marks to OE officials in aiding their planning efforts, but feel themselves to be restricted by the stipulations accompanying categorical programs, the lack of sufficient lead time, and the lateness and tenuousness of funds that filter down from Washington.[23] However, with rare exception, it can be argued that SEAs fail to blunt the impact of these federal constraints because they have not taken the initiative to establish comprehensive planning structures or to recruit planners for key SEA positions.[24]

Goal Setting and Federal Aid

The federal government's policy preferences are not always those of many of the states. As Sufrin has noted, "even if the educational ideals of the state capitals are the same as those of Washington . . . the states in their wisdom need not always agree with the value judgments of the federal government with respect to the effectiveness of additional expenditures."[25] Thus it could be argued, as did many survey respondents, that federal funds should be dispensed in the form of general aid because state-level policy-makers and SEAs are more sensitive to their states' priority educational needs. However, there is a shortcoming in this logic. The SEAs have been notoriously reluctant to establish goals, particularly those that are statewide, clearly defined and comprehensive in scope, and based upon needs information gathered from across the state.[26]

Of course, it is quite risky for agencies to clearly state and publicly announce their goals. Once goals are announced it is probable that state legislators and governors will demand specific assessment information and maybe even seek to establish close and formal supervisory mechanisms over SEA activities. But there is little to indicate that this is the situation confronting the SEAs. That is, it is not a question of SEAs setting goals and then withholding them from scrutiny by policy makers. Rather it appears to be a case of little or no effort to set goals, at least by most SEAs. An ERIC review of the literature on SEAs has found that "the general theme of most of the studies and articles is that state departments of education do not play as great a role as they should in development and implementation of new, innovative educational policies."[27] In fact, as a result of visiting many of these agencies, Nix has concluded that "there is still considerable confusion . . . among state department personnel regarding the meaning of the terms goals, objectives, needs and programs. The on-site visits to state departments of education were often characterized by different persons within the same department of education using these terms in quite different senses."[28]

The SEAs' performance in setting internal goals makes it somewhat doubtful that they can respond adequately to demands that statewide priorities be set. As noted earlier, the program level is where most SEA planning takes place. This is also true of goal setting. It is at this level that specific demands for performance are made and administrators are held responsible for their actions. Thus it is not surprising that planning projects such as those funded through ESEA Title V have not moved SEAs closer to establishing comprehensive goals for intra-agency activities. Title V coordinators in both New York and California have commented that funds in their agencies were dispersed piecemeal with no overall priorities set by top-level SEA officials.

It has not been a specific responsibility of SEAs to establish statewide needs or develop educational goals. But the increasing policy initiatives and resource inputs of both the states and the federal government are forcing SEAs to move into such activities. The question is not whether they should, but whether they can respond adequately.

The study by Nix, which included interviews with leaders of six SEAs and a survey of those in 25 others, indicates that most SEAs do not appear to have been able to translate the results of needs assessments into specific goals or priorities.[29] Recently a few SEAs have begun to make the effort. Maryland, for example, has conducted a survey to assess the perceptions of both teachers and the general public regarding educational goals that should be pursued. The survey has led to the formulation of educational priorities in that state, (i.e., career education, early childhood education, human relations, and reading) and several subunits of the Maryland SEA have begun to develop special programs in these areas.[30]

Michigan has moved to establish statewide goals based on a "comprehensive planning-needs assessment program."[31] Employing ESEA Title III funds, the Michigan SEA's needs-assessment survey focused on student groups most in need of concentrated educational efforts and the development of goals and specific program areas that should be emphasized.[32]

In California the legislature has played a key role, passing a measure to establish "broad minimum standards and guidelines for educational programs" based on "stated philosophy, goals and objectives."[33] School districts have been asked to voluntarily establish local goals that can be used by the legislature and the SEA to develop state-level goals and to formulate legislation that is congruent with these goals.

The New York SEA has attempted to survey overall educational needs and has developed tentative goals. Its first attempt at overall planning for the direction of education was in 1961[34] but it was not until ESEA Title III resources became available that it began in earnest to set priorities for resource allocation. The initial outcome of this survey, a list of 19 major concerns, was reduced and restated several times. The SEA's resultant position paper was then debated by educators throughout the state with the hope that a set of goals could be agreed upon and used as a basis for future state-level resource allocations for education.[35]

As tentative as such efforts are, they represent the first attempts by SEAs to assess needs and establish goals to guide educational governance. But the fact that they are still the exception rather than the rule indicates that the federal government's attempt to have SEAs set comprehensive goals to guide planning has fallen short of intent thus far. The ways in which SEAs have deployed ESEA Title V funds is not very encouraging. Neither are the SEAs' responses to the requirement that they file state plans with OE before they can participate in most federal programs.* Among other things, state plans are normally expected to include statements regarding how SEAs will set priorities on project application approvals. In reality, however, the value of state plans is questionable. In the opinion of many OE officials, most SEA state plans are paper exercises and a waste of time. In short, whether due to constraints related to stringent categorical aid programs or to a lack of SEA initiative, the fact is that most state agencies have not set long-range comprehensive goals.

---

*ESEA Title I is an exception to the state plan routine. Funds are targeted to the county level so SEAs have only been required to "assure" OE of their intent to control expenditures.

IV/Internal Activities: Organizational Practices and Task Attainment

T o this point attention has been limited to a description of the federal government's intervention in education and the SEAs' internal responses to that intervention. In particular the focus has been on SEA implementation of regulatory and developmental tasks related to administration of NDEA and ESEA titles. The intent of this chapter is to explore SEA practices that may help to clarify why they chose to respond as they have. Two organizational practices in particular seem to be relevant. The first that will be considered is SEA personnel practices, including recruitment and retention of staff. The second that will be considered is the way that federal programs are administered and co-ordinated within SEA organizational structures.

Personnel Practices

Activities associated with federal program administration have required most SEAs to more than double their staff components during the 1960s. In addition to sheer numbers of personnel, for many SEAs the federal initiative represented an excellent opportunity to recruit highly skilled staff members and to upgrade the skills of those already there. Such, however, does not appear to have occurred.

Recruitment

Recruitment has become a major concern for SEAs since their roles increased due to expanding state and federal involvement in education. Campbell and Mazzoni note that SEA task areas that demand "increased attention include planning, research, development, and evaluation. Each of these areas will require an expertise which is not often found in the personnel ordinarily recruited to state departments in the past."[1] This conclusion parallels an earlier finding by Kirby and Tollman that SEAs have attempted to meet changing needs "with the same personnel, or more of the same kind of personnel [and] . . . they provide virtually no evidence that they have been considering procedures which might develop new sources, new career programs, or new inducements to attract top educators with a variety of talents." The "same kind of personnel" means staff members "who have lived their lives in the rural areas of the states they serve; who have gone to State teachers' college and perhaps the State university; who had begun careers as professional educators, generally in rural schools, before entering the department; and who had been invited to join the department by another member of the State Department of Education."[2]

In 1974 a 12-state survey by Branson found that 60% of the administrators in those SEAs were recruited by means of personal contacts with others already in these agencies.[3] Furthermore, the previous experience of 31% of these SEA administrators was limited to rural school districts of less than 1000 students, and more than 80% were recruited from in-state positions.[4] Nyquist has characterized such predominant SEA practices as "intellectual incest."[5] This may be, but they are representative of long-standing SEA recruitment procedures and, since SEAs have historically been staffed in this manner, it is not likely that such practices will be changed in a short time.

The result, in most SEAs, is a rather homogenous staff. As Murphy has concluded, "Homogeniety, of course, is not the same as incompetence. It may tend, however, to establish an inbred, insular attitude and approach which probably are resistant to new ideas, innovations or acceptance of employees from different backgrounds."[6] Whether these harsh indictments are justified is not as important as the probability that so long as SEA staff are selected from among the ranks of those they are to oversee, they can hardly be expected to have much enthusiasm for critically regulating school districts' activities or pressuring them to try new approaches.

Still there are the exceptions indicating that SEAs can devise other responses to staff-recruitment needs. For example, the NDEA Bureau in the California SEA is staffed with professionals whose career backgrounds are much like the patterns described above;

from teaching, to graduate study, to rural school district administrative posts, and to the state level. However, the very same SEA, spurred on by the state legislature, mounted a unique staff-recruitment program to meet the administrative requirements of ESEA Title I. The then director of the program, Wilson Riles, was given a free hand to recruit personnel and initially selected key bureau chiefs from among SEA staff members whom he knew personally and respected for their knowledge about compensatory education as well as for their probable acceptance by the target population; of the five top posts, three were filled by minority group members. To fill the 60 staff positions authorized to get the program started, he purposely bypassed established SEA personnel recruitment procedures, and searched the state for people with particular skills in compensatory education. Looking back on the effort he concluded:

> If you've got the people who can operate a program, the program operates, I don't care what kind of chart you draw. Flexibility allowing me to choose staff was critical. I only chose four out of many departmental applicants. We are dealing in an area to which the school system has been insensitive. You don't just grab up someone and make him a consultant on the disadvantaged. I brought in those I wanted from within and without the department. I couldn't have done it without separate division status. It enabled me to avoid the established bureaucracy.[7]

In New York an attempt to recruit unique personnel was deliberately planned by top SEA decision-makers. Former Commissioner James Allen Jr. and his deputies purposefully set out to find recruits, especially for top-level positions, who might not have had experience as professional educators but who had established reputations as skillful planners and doers. For example, the position of director of the Long Range Planning Office was filled by raiding another state agency, the influential and highly respected Division of the Budget. As a result of planning experience in his Budget position, the director had insights into means of generating planning efforts in the SEA that he probably could not have obtained as a schoolman. Several other key personnel positions were also filled from outside the traditional talent pool. These new staff members are not committed to the status quo, as are many of the SEA recruits drawn from school district sources.

These examples indicate that traditional personnel hiring practices can be unfrozen by the purposeful efforts of SEA leaders or through external pressures from policy-making bodies such as state legislatures. In the long run, it is probably to the SEAs' advantage to take the initiative because if they do not, legislatures and governors probably will.

Retention

Professional personnel do not remain in SEAs for long periods of time. In Massachusetts "during the 18 months between July, 1968, and January, 1970, there were 59 resignations by professional staff of the Department. . . . Most of these people were promising young educators with about 14 to 16 months of service, just the kind of men and women so desperately needed to give the Department the thrust it requires."[8] Even in New York, perhaps the most prestigious of the SEAs, there has been a "vacancy rate that has remained rather consistently at fifteen percent."[9] Other SEAs have had similar difficulty retaining staff.[10] OE data show that "20 percent of [SEA] personnel left their departments for one reason or another" during 1968. Most telling, "three-fourths of the present staffs have been in their jobs less than 3 years."[11]

There are two factors in particular that constrain SEA efforts to retain staff. First, many federally supported SEA positions have a tenuous funding base. State legislatures and governors are reticent to give permanence to these staff positions because they fear the states will have to continue financial support for them if federal money is withdrawn. In addition, when the federal budget is constricted, categorical aid program funding suffers and SEAs must cut back on staff support. SEA administrators have long maintained that support for the professional staff required to manage federal programs has been insufficient even in normal times. When there are budgetary cutbacks, as there were in 1970, the problem becomes enormously aggravated. Programs have been initiated and commitments have been made; tasks remain at least constant while support dollars for co-ordinators and administrators are withdrawn. For example, the director of the ESEA Title II program in New York felt that the 1970 cutbacks left her with funds for only "routine administration, that's all. In actuality the unit has suffered by loss of personnel who have been removed to other units because there are no federal funds to support them."

The second factor is that civil service rules and regulations rarely take into account the special needs of SEAs. Educational specialists, at least until recently, have been in short supply because of the enormous expansion in the education sector that followed the baby-boom years of the 1940s and 1950s. At the school district level these professionals have been able to negotiate for attractive salaries with minimal constraints on their managerial freedom. At the state level, however, there are civil service restrictions on salaries and limitations on job specifications. As a result SEAs are in a poor competitive position and SEA staff members are tempted to move into school district positions. In Massachusetts "senior supervisors" earned between $10,000 and $13,000 per year in 1970 while superintendents and principals were typically earning $5,000 to $10,000 *above* these figures.[12] In fact, the average salary for all professional, administrative, and technical personnel in SEAs across the country that year was only $12,162.[13]

It is difficult for SEAs to recruit and retain experienced professionals in the prime of their careers under these conditions. For the main part, only the inexperienced and low-paid young or the very experienced and retiring old can be attracted to SEA positions. Given these conditions, it is not surprising that SEA staff members whose positions are funded through federal programs such as the NDEA and the ESEA are often tempted to look elsewhere for employment when opportunities arise.

There are, of course, examples of continuity in SEA staffing for federal programs despite these constraints. In California the NDEA Bureau has been able to retain key staff and turnover has generally been low. Similarly, in both New York and California key ESEA Title I staff remained in their posts long enough to firmly establish these programs.

However, once SEAs overcome initial constraints and are able to retain key staff members, they must deal with threats from different quarters. If personnel are competent other agencies can be expected to try to lure them away, a problem not unique to SEAs. Raids on organizations' executives are common in both the public and the private sectors. But the SEAs, given their initial recruitment constraints, are in a particularly vulnerable position when they lose their few exceptional administrators. OE is constantly on the alert for educational administrators who can help to manage federal programs. School districts, state agencies, and even other SEAs often recruit from among successful SEA administrators.

Staffing Adaptations

Given recruitment and retention constraints, how do SEAs manage to fill their staffing needs? Some cynics might conclude that SEAs respond by hiring retired superintendents or educators unwanted elsewhere. But this is, at best, only one of the SEAs' responses. While no SEA appears to be exceptionally successful in attracting and retaining well-qualified professionals, there are some recruitment and retention practices that seem to have potential. To begin, some SEAs challenge their states' civil service or personnel boards' rulings by developing unique job classifications that allow them to recruit personnel they could not otherwise attract. For example, the California State Personnel Board tries to restrain executive agencies from hiring temporary personnel. Although programs such as Title V of ESEA provide resources that can be used to hire consultants on a temporary basis, the SEA must first gain approval from the board. The SEA's personnel unit was able to get necessary clearance by inventing a new job classification, "Educational Project Specialists," that had no permanent status attached.

Second, it may be possible to attract and retain qualified personnel if they view position openings as a challenge and identify closely with the goals of the program. As noted, three of the top five officials in the California SEA's Office of Compensatory Education were recruited from minority ranks to administer the aspects of ESEA Title I that focus on the educationally deprived, many of whom are minority group children.

Third, once staff are recruited, in-service programs can be initiated to improve their substantive knowledge and managerial skills.[14] Frequently federal dollars reserved for SEA administrative activities can be legitimately used to support staff improvement projects. The New York ESEA Title II program director has routinely opted to reserve five percent of the administrative dollars at her disposal for in-service training programs. Such practices can do much to upgrade SEA staff skills so that improved services can be offered to school districts. Unfortunately such in-service practices are far from universal. OE's annual report for 1970 shows that only 24 states spent ESEA Title V funds for "enlarging staff competencies through initiation or expansion of inservice training."[15]

Finally, there is the possibility of "doubling-up" or "piggybacking" responsibilites. If program needs cannot be met because of insufficient staff, due either to fiscal constraints or to the shortage of able candidates, program administrators can turn to other staff members in their own SEAs. The New York ESEA Title II unit director, in another instance, had decided to carry out a statewide survey of school library services and did not want to abandon this objective when she lost staff because of cuts in federal appropriations. She discovered that she could simply append survey items to the SEA's annual school district information gathering instrument. In this manner she was able to obtain data from *all* school districts and free tabulating assistance from the SEA's computer personnel.

In summary, personnel difficulties have constrained SEA efforts to accomplish tasks associated with federally funded education programs. Restrictive civil service requirements and the unwillingness of state legislators and governors to provide job security for administrators of federal programs have been particularly detrimental to the SEAs' efforts to recruit and retain qualified personnel. There are recruiting and retention practices that SEAs can employ to at least partially overcome this problem, but such efforts are still the exception to the rule.

Organizational Structures: Co-ordination vs. Concentration

Many states did not begin to develop categorical education programs until quite recently. In effect, for most SEAs the NDEA and the ESEA represented the first time since the passage of the Smith-Hughes Act of 1917 (vocational education) that they have been required to organize, implement, maintain, and evaluate specific educational programs. As these agencies have grown and taken on new tasks, they have been hard-pressed to design administrative structures that can account for both the co-ordination and the concentration required to achieve intended purposes. In Massachusetts, for example, the SEA was hardly prepared to co-ordinate federal programs. There had been little if any prior co-ordination attempted in the agency. In fact, according to Iannaccone, "in most divisions, it is the bureau level which does things, and each bureau within a division tends to work by itself. Horizontal linkages are less important, if that is possible. The mesh of the department is made of personal links."[16]

Co-ordination is necessary to assure that differentiated subunits work in harmony to serve overall organizational purposes. At the same time, concentration of effort is required to assure that specific program needs are met. Balancing these two organizational needs becomes one of the SEA leaders' most important tasks. If co-ordination is achieved at the cost of concentration, then intended aims of individual programs may not be met. On the other hand, if programs are managed along totally independent unit lines, SEAs may promote feudal bureaucratic subunits that make it most difficult to maintain an overall agency thrust.

The struggle to attain agency co-ordination without losing concentration of effort is not unique to SEAs. Every organization must design structures that assure a balance between the co-ordination required to achieve comprehensive efforts and the concentration needed to assure that immediate tasks are fulfilled. One thing is certain: as organizations increase the scope of their activities, the potential for job specialization and task concentration also grows. In such a situation it is important to devise controls to assure that the work of specialists is co-ordinated so that desired outcomes can be attained. This is no easy task, especially in organizations such as SEAs that are dominated by professionals who often resist centralized controls.

Federal aid has not created the SEAs' co-ordination *vs.* concentration dilemma, but it certainly has reinforced it. As a major study conducted in 1969 concluded, "both state and federal financial programs for education have suffered from a lack of careful and comprehensive planning. In 1966-67 there were at least 441 funds making up the school finance program of the 50 states. . . . The primary reason for this situation is an obvious lack of planning and evaluation of finance designs. This lack of planning is vividly demonstrated by the over-abundance of uncoordinated federal programs as well as state programs."[17] An example of this is the Economic Opportunity Act of 1964 (Public Law 88-452), which authorizes grants for programs that may also be eligible for ESEA Title I funding. In fact, a review by the Office of Economic Opportunity and OE concluded that *28* different kinds of programs could be eligible for either grant![18]

Everyone endorses the desirability of co-ordinating federal programs to avoid overlaps and vacuums and to maximize potential outcomes. The President advocates and Congress debates the desirability of general aid and revenue-sharing programs so that the states can devise comprehensive and co-ordinated plans for the employment of federal funds. State legislatures press SEAs to co-ordinate administration of federal programs so that school districts can develop consolidated project applications. State boards of education and top-level SEA administrators frequently decry the lack of co-ordination of federal programs and seek means to alleviate the problem. What is the result of all this rhetoric? To answer this question we shall look at the SEA co-ordination *vs.* concentration dilemma as it occurs at two levels: within individual programs and between complementary programs. Most SEAs are presently wrestling with the co-ordination *vs.* concentration issue at both of these levels.[19]

Within Individual Programs

Managing federal programs in compartmentalized, single-unit administrative structures can promote concentration of effort but may detract from overall SEA co-ordination and planning. In contrast, assigning federal program functions to previously established units (such as placing evaluation components with an agency's system-wide evaluation unit) enhances the potential for co-ordination and planning, but can detract from necessary program concentration. The responses of SEAs to this problem are far from clear. In fact, even within single SEAs there are often extensive variations to be found in administrative arrangements for federal programs.

To illustrate, we will explore the administrative arrangements devised by the SEAs in New York and California for ESEA Titles I, II, III, and V. Several patterns emerge from a review of Figure 12. The California administrative pattern appears to enhance concentration by assuring that all bureaus performing tasks related to a single federal program come from within a single division; the New York administrative pattern appears less clear, functions are divided across divisions for ESEA Titles I and II, but co-ordinated in a fashion similar to California's for ESEA Titles III and V.

California's SEA has devised an administrative pattern that assures maximum concentration of *ESEA Title I* efforts* while New York's SEA has chosen to disperse the program through existing units. The California SEA's single unit has responsibility for administration of state-mandated compensatory education programs as well as for Title I. Even the physical layout of the office space for the California program stresses concentration of effort. When a school-district official arrives to seek funds he finds an outer door that opens onto a long corridor containing five office doors. In order,

---

*California's SEA probably would not have chosen this pattern except for the fact that the state legislature intervened to mandate an administrative structure. This intervention will be discussed in Chapter V.

FIGURE 12.   ADMINISTRATIVE PATTERNS FOR ESEA TITLES IN THE
CALIFORNIA AND NEW YORK SEAS (1970)

The California SEA

ESEA Title	Division	Bureau	Program Approval and Consultation Functions	Evaluation Functions	Fiscal Functions
I	Compensatory Education	Compensatory Education Program Development	X		
		Compensatory Education Evaluation and Research		X	
		Compensatory Education Fiscal Management			X
II	Instruction	Audio-Visual and School Library Education	X	X	
		National Defense Education Act Administration			X
III	Instruction	Program Planning and Development	X	X	X
V	Attached to Deputy Supt. of Public Instruction (Title V Co-ordinator)	Any successfully applying divisions	X		
		Associate Supt.'s Office (Title V Co-ordinator)		X	X

			Program Approval and Consultation Functions	*Evaluation Functions*	*Fiscal Functions*
ESEA Title	*Division*	*Bureau*			
I	Education for the Disadvantaged	Program Unit	X		
		Field Service Unit	X		
	Instructional Services	Instructional Unit	X		
		Evaluation Unit		X	
	Educational Finance and Management Services	Fiscal Units			X
II	Instructional Services	School Libraries	X	X	
	Educational Finance and Management Services	Fiscal Units			X
III	Attached to Exec. Deputy Commissioner's Office	Center for Planning and Innovation	X	X	X
V	Attached to Exec. Deputy Commissioner's Office (Title V Co-ordinator is the Asst. Commissioner for Administrative Services)	Any successfully applying divisions	X		
		Exec. Deputy Commissioner's Office (Title V Co-ordinator)		X	X

The New York SEA

they are: the general administrative offices, Community Services, Program Development, Program Evaluation and, finally, at the far end of the hall, Finance. After announcing his arrival in the general offices he proceeds down the long hall, door by door, to gain approval of his district's project. If he can satisfy the Community Services staff that the project will involve target-area parents he is then ushered into Program Development where he must convince the staff of the logic of the project's objectives and procedures. If he passes this check point he proceeds to Evaluation where he must assure staff members that his district has a clear and feasible plan for judging the results of the proposed project. Finally, assuming approval has been given by all units, he arrives at Finance to arrange transfer of funds so the school district can initiate the program.

At least in part because of its concentrated effort California has frequently been referred to as a leader in compensatory education.[20] However, there has been a high cost. The Office of Compensatory Education has been isolated within the SEA. Communication of objectives and procedures across unit lines has been minimal because the California SEA's administrative pattern for ESEA Title I made it difficult for compensatory-education advocates in the SEA to play a role in larger SEA planning and goal-setting efforts.*

In New York not only has Title I been parcelled out through existing units in the SEA, but administration of the state's own urban-education program was totally divorced from that of Title I until 1970 when it was finally transferred to the Education for the Disadvantaged Division. The decision to disperse program elements throughout the agency's structure has made it necessary to establish a monitoring system to assure that the pieces all fit together in the end. As a result, while the New York Title I effort has not gained the national recognition that California's has, it has increased the potential for a more comprehensive SEA-wide approach to education for the disadvantaged by involving top-level SEA personnel in planning and program monitoring. In all probability, the New York legislature would not have seriously considered a unique state-level special aid program for urban education had it not been for the wide-spread interest and involvement of key SEA leaders in compensatory education.[21]

In California, control over *ESEA Title II* has been assigned to

---

*This difficulty may have been overcome since the former director of the ESEA Title I program, Wilson Riles, was elected superintendent of public instruction.

an existing unit, the Audio-visual and School Library Education Bureau, as one of its many program responsibilities. In New York, the program has been assigned to a self-contained unit, the Bureau of School Libraries. Being able to concentrate on Title II issues, the New York SEA's unit appears to have made great progress toward long-range planning. It has conducted statewide surveys and established priority needs that Title II projects must serve. An OE administrator who monitors ESEA Title II activity noted that, at least in part because of its concentrated effort, New York's program has had good results.

In California, *ESEA Title III* administration is assigned to the Program Planning and Development unit within the Division of Instruction. In New York it is administered by the Center for Planning and Innovation, a unit attached to the Executive Deputy Commissioner's Office. With high visibility and a direct link to key decision-makers, staff in the New York unit are employed to support the SEA's effort to co-ordinate department-wide activities. In fact, the priority goal setting effort in the New York SEA described earlier was given its initial impetus by this unit. The director of the unit, who carries the title of assistant commissioner, played a key leadership role in the effort. Such possibilities have never existed in California because the Program Planning and Development unit is buried several levels down in that SEA's organizational structure. Furthermore, the California unit has also been plagued by rapid turnover of key personnel and by the state legislature's successful efforts to supercede the SEA's authority by setting policy for Title III program operation.[22]

ESEA Title V is supervised at the top organizational level in both SEAs. Still there are important differences. In California the Title V co-ordinator manages a small separate unit (himself and one secretary), but he has little if any continuing contact with key SEA leaders. Actually, for several years the California pattern was to administer ESEA Title V as one of many functions within a bureau. This meant even less influence for the co-ordinator than is presently the case. In New York the co-ordinating role has been assigned as an additional duty to an assistant commissioner. The New York co-ordinator is not able to turn his full attention to Title V, but his high position within the SEA gives him the influence base, the legitimacy, and the visibility required to assure that projects serve overall ends. However, while New York's structure *potentially* can enable it to so employ Title V, this has not happened. The disinclination of division leaders to co-ordinate activites even within their own units, the declining federal resources attached to Title V, and the lack of fully developed and clearly written state-level educational goals mitigate against this possibility. In both SEAs, because of the lack of high-level planning, Title V dollars have been diverted to the more mundane but immediate needs of organizational maintenance.

Across Programs

SEAs can, but rarely do, create comprehensive packages out of the myriad of programs they oversee. One of their less successful responses has been to create subcommittees of state boards of education. An example of this strategy is California's Federal Aid to Education subcommittee. Consisting of four board members, the committee is responsible for reviewing agency proposals regarding federal programs and for bringing policy recommendations to the full board for action. However, the committee is swamped with a heavy load of ongoing SEA proposals so maintenance activities dominate the brief time available to it. As the board secretary observed, because it only meets occasionally and its work load is so demanding "there is absolutely no effort discernible" that the committee deals with co-ordination of federal programs.

With little in the way of guidance from OE or their own state-level governing bodies, SEA officials often attempt to establish their own co-ordination of federal programs. Most successful have been their efforts to actively link the administration of complementary programs together. Because ESEA Title II can be used to provide resource materials for school libraries, many SEAs have decided to administer it in units they had established earlier for NDEA Title III, a program that can also be used for such purposes. Similarly, where functions of individual programs are divided among existing units, many SEAs set up co-ordinating structures to provide overall program guidance and to act as links with OE. A shortcoming in this approach is that it is difficult to get staff members who are attached to these diverse units to view themselves as a team working toward common ends. To promote the team notion, staff meetings in most such SEA arrangements are held on a regular basis under the auspices of the co-ordinating unit. In practice, however, this strategy rarely works because individuals, having demanding schedules and primary loyalties to other units, find it difficult to commit themselves to the co-ordinating unit's program planning sessions.

Other arrangements that depend upon voluntary cooperation across program lines are even less viable. In California, for example, the SEA attempted to co-ordinate all existing and future federal programs within its NDEA Bureau. But the agency encountered external problems when the state legislature mandated a separate organizational structure for ESEA Title I. Given the constraints of separate organizational structures imposed by the legislature, the SEA responded by establishing an internal "Department Committee for Co-ordinating Federal Programs." This committee was formed in 1966 to provide the state board and the superintendent with information needed to make policy decisions regarding federal programs. As might be expected, results fell far short of the intent. For a start, there is no representation of top-level SEA officials on the committee. Furthermore, due to resistance from the agency's federal program directors, the committee's work has been limited to problems that are non-threatening and low level (such as discrepancies in pay for consultants and variations in program application forms).

There is little if any discussion regarding long-range planning or meaningful co-ordination of federal programs. As a result the committee, after an initial flurry of activity, has tended to meet only when particular committee members have expressed a specific need to confer. New York had a similar co-ordinating committee, but according to one top official it has since "been lost in the woodwork." Finding no interest across program lines beyond attempts to consolidate application forms, the committee has ceased to function. These dismal results are not unique to California and New York. In a recent study Nix found that the impact of SEA co-ordinating committees is severely limited: "There were no visible evidences that any of these groups were producing disciplined, long range plans for the state department or any of its major parts."[23]

The same absence of co-ordination is evident in the management of complementary federal and state categorical education programs, where such state-level programs have been initiated. Soon after passage of the ESEA, the California legislative analyst prepared the following status report regarding the SEAs' co-ordination difficulties:

> Presently the department is responsible for the supervision and coordination of 14 state and federal categorical aid programs. These individual programs are administered by over 10 separate bureaus and divisions with no arrangements for the joint approval of local programs

which might complement each other. This makes it difficult for the department to encourage the most efficiently organized local projects. For example, the Bureau of National Defense Education, within the Division of Instruction, is engaged in many programs designed to improve the instruction of reading and English in the public school system, yet it has nothing at all to do with the administration of the Miller-Unruh Basic Reading Act (a state program) or with the administration of the 1965 Elementary and Secondary Education Act which includes as one of its major components the improvement of reading skills for poverty pupils.[24]

Recognizing this difficulty, the legislature moved to assure that ESEA Title I and the state's compensatory education programs would be co-ordinated within a single SEA unit, the Office of Compensatory Education. Even with this forethought it has remained quite difficult for the office to co-ordinate the many applications it receives for state and federal compensatory-education programs. Because it continues to find that school districts resist establishing major overall objectives in this substantive area, the office in 1974 decided to require that local officials develop consolidated applications that promise to employ both federal and state resources for compensatory education programs.

Identifiable Structural Responses

The discussion regarding organizational designs for administration of federal programs indicates that once differentiating structures are established it becomes quite difficult to induce unit directors to voluntarily co-ordinate activities across program lines. In fact, it might be concluded that SEAs are "loose confederations of relatively independent program components."[25]

In defense of SEAs there are external constraints, such as organizational structures mandated by state legislatures and the highly restrictive categorical packaging of federal aid. In addition, OE tends to establish new units almost every time a new aid program is approved by Congress, which makes it a rather poor role-model of a co-ordinated system. While there are such external constraints, co-ordination problems in SEAs are probably due more to individual program directors' fears that their domains will be encroached upon if they cooperate across unit lines. For different reasons, both aggressively confident administrators who believe they have devised the most appropriate approaches and administrators who are quite unsure of their effectiveness probably resist sharing their units' plans and problems with other SEA administrators. The former resist because they want no interference with successful program management and the latter, because they fear being exposed as incompetent.

Given these external and internal constraints, many SEA leaders find it difficult to attain the balance required between concentration of program effort and co-ordination of agency activities toward larger ends. They do make an effort but their efforts usually fall short of their expectations because SEAs are not well designed to cope with this difficult situation. The systems model presented in Chapter II stressed the fact that the way in which tasks are processed is directly affected by organizational decisions regarding authority, control, and reward structures. In the SEAs, decisions regarding these structures have tended to result in resistance to co-ordination of efforts.

SEA *authority structures* usually include at least three tiers; the superintendent and his immediate subordinates, the divisions, and the bureaus within divisions. This hierarchical structure tends to retard lateral communication across divisions, especially at the lower levels of these agencies where most programs are administered. Thus administrators of complementary programs can plan and carry out their tasks almost totally isolated from each other. Priorities and administrative procedures across programs are rarely discussed, especially when they are assigned to bureaus that report to different divisions. To compound the situation, administrators assigned to federal programs may view OE as their real source of authority, because regulations and guidelines require their reporting to it concerning program matters. In fact, it is possible that they work with OE officials more frequently than they do with superiors in their own agencies. As a result they may view OE as more important for their job security and for maintenance of their program units, both of which depend upon continuing resource inputs from the federal level, not from the state level.

As to *control structures,* SEA rules and regulations regarding federal program administration have been slow to appear. Most SEAs have been sorely challenged just to stay one step ahead of the expanding federal input: recruiting staff and devising new patterns of program administration have taken much of their time. As a result, SEA guidelines often borrow freely from federal guidelines and state-designated rules and regulations for federal programs are just now beginning to emerge. A major difficulty blocking this effort is that SEAs are populated by personnel who, as professionals, can be expected to resist rules and regulations either for themselves or for school district administrators. In organizations dominated by professionals, the preference tends to be toward self-discipline and it is most difficult for organizational leaders to impose hierarchical controls, especially regarding performance data from specialized units. However, unless the system can successfully establish means of getting such data and comparing them with expectations there can be no assurance that subunits will work cooperatively to achieve organizational ends.

Finally, SEA *reward structures* have worked in opposition to co-ordinated efforts. Most SEAs assign specific tasks to staff members and reward them, by promotion, salary raises, or other means, according to the extent that results meet task expectations. There is little if any serious effort to distribute rewards to program directors on the basis of overall SEA performance. Thus it is to the advantage of administrators to secure maximum control over units they direct to minimize interference in moving their programs toward intended outcomes. Within concentrated frameworks, program administrators can enjoy the status and authority of autonomous unit directors. If, on the other hand, they share responsibility or even information they may be required to modify program designs or program objectives to satisfy others. Openness *may* lead to better results, but program administrators are understandably wary of upsetting the structures and processes they prefer and have worked so hard to establish. They might even conclude that with program co-ordination they could be shuffled into subordinate positions in larger and more comprehensive units.

In short, there are many reasons that unit directors tend to favor concentrated administrative structures and resist administrative patterns that promote co-ordinated efforts across federal-program lines. There is little doubt that program administrators will continue to promote highly focused, individual units for categorical aid administration as long as they see such structures as progammatically effective and personally rewarding. It remains to be seen whether leaders in the SEAs can unfreeze the present situation by altering authority structures or by modifying reward and control structures.

Summary of Internal Responses

SEA tasks have been viewed as reactive, or regulatory, and

proactive, or developmental. For the regulatory tasks of auditing and evaluating, SEAs continue to function in much the same manner as they did prior to recent federal intitiatives. The use of federal resources for improvement of regulatory-task performance has been constrained by preferences of SEAs to use their limited resources to hire subject area specialists instead of auditors and evaluators. Also, SEA staff have been unwilling to closely scrutinize their counterparts at the school district level because they recognize the need to maintain good relationships with district officials, even at the cost of achieving program purposes.

Having had little experience with developmental tasks prior to the 1960s most SEAs have been hard-pressed to improve their performance in a relatively short time span. A pervasive shortcoming is that most planning activities are concentrated at the program level, and there is little co-ordination or direction of comprehensive planning from the top SEA echelons.

There may be external constraints on planning for federal programs, such as lack of lead time, late funding, and highly specified objectives, but planning can still be carried out on a comprehensive basis. SEA officials argue that federal aid should not be distributed with specific program objectives because goals are best set at the state level, but few SEAs have even begun to assess educational needs upon which comprehensive statewide goals should be based.

SEAs are constrained in their accomplishment of regulatory and developmental tasks because of personnel problems and organizational design shortcomings. As to personnel, SEA staff rosters, in most instances, have more than doubled, but new staff members tend to be recruited from traditional talent pool sources. That is, SEA staff are still selected from among in-state administrators in rural school districts. As a result, they tend to view tasks in much the same way as their predecessors. Where SEAs have selected staff from other sources, either voluntarily or as a result of external pressures, there has usually been more interest in fashioning unique responses to meet the challenges posed by federal-grant administration.

An additional personnel difficulty is the SEAs' inability to retain staff due to salary scales that are low in comparison to those of competitive organizations, rigid civil service requirements, and lack of job security associated with federal-program administration. SEAs that have done well in staff retention are those that are able to influence civil service boards to modify job classifications, provide in-service education to upgrade staff once appointed, make full use of SEA resources to accomplish tasks, and seek recruits who identify with the objectives of specific programs.

Organizational design problems that plague SEAs as they have responded to federal inputs center upon stresses created by organizational needs for both co-ordination and concentration. The SEAs attempt to co-ordinate programs to assure that overall organizational purposes are met. At the same time they promote concentration of efforts so that short-range purposes associated with individual programs can be fulfilled. This co-ordination *vs.* concentration dilemma, within single programs and between complementary programs, is a particular problem for those SEAs that had not had much previous experience in the management of categorical aid programs.

SEA organizational structures tend to inhibit comprehensive efforts. SEA authority structures often retard communication and co-ordination; control structures have not been sufficiently developed to deal with the needs created by the federal input, and rewards usually go to program-management entrepreneurs who make all decisions themselves rather than accept the risks associated with cooperating across program lines.

In short, there have been a few SEAs that have moved as a result of the federal impact to change and upgrade their performance, but for most, either the need to do so has not become apparent or they have not been willing or able to make the necessary adjustments. If SEAs continue to resist modifying their internal activities it is probable that governors, state legislatures, and Congress, will *require* them to do so. To explore this potential, in Chapter V we will turn to the ramifications of the SEAs administration of federal programs as it relates to external organizations.

V/External Relations

All organizations establish some processes for dealing with the needs, role preferences, and group affiliations of their members. They must also design rational system and subsystem authority and control and reward structures that can cushion the shock of introducing new or modified purposes and processes. However at the organization-environment interface, structures and behavior are less clearly understood and frequently less amenable to unilateral manipulation. There are organizations that make demands, provide resources, accept outputs, and perform tasks vital to the work of the SEAs. In this chapter we will explore SEA responses to challenges posed by administering the NDEA and the ESEA and their modifying and expanding relations with these other organizations. After a brief discussion of interorganizational relations as an area of study, the focus will turn to a review of SEA relationships with "organization-sets"[1] in their environment. These organization-sets will be categorized as *superior* or *subordinate* in the line of authority, and *outside* the line of authority. Strategies of influence employed in these relationships will be emphasized and comparisons and contrasts will be made to help clarify variations in the SEAs' responses.

Interorganizational Analysis

The study of interorganizational relations is just beginning to emerge as important to the understanding of organizational life.[2] Even by the close of the 1960s interorganizational behavior was still not an important focus for behavioral scientists. Interorganizational relations were not subjected to the depth of analysis given to intraorganizational relations. In fact it was not until 1969 that a major conference was finally held with the sole purpose being to bring interested behavioral scientists together to pool their knowledge regarding this emerging research area.[3]

79

Currently, interest in interorganizational analysis is growing rapidly. The recent emphasis within the behavioral sciences on systems theory, borrowed from the natural sciences,[4] has prompted organizational analysts to give greater consideration to the importance of environmental factors such as demand-and-resource inputs and output-acceptance as these factors shape organizational behavior and structures. When organizations are viewed as subsystems of the larger society that they serve and depend on for inputs, the impact that environmental constraints and potentials can hold for them becomes more clear.

The rapid rate of change being encountered by social structures has also lent urgency to interorganizational study. The ever-increasing rate of change, or "future shock," in the environment affects organizations in much the same way as it does individuals. As long as the environment is stable, relationships remain relatively static. However, as Lawrence and Lorsch note, the "complexity of information" required by organizations increases when there is a "high degree of uncertainty and change in the relevant part of the environment."[5] When demands change or increase and when resources become more difficult to attain or shift in their locus, organizations must be able to make appropriate modifications or risk loss of input-support and output-acceptance from their environments.

Most organizations can ill-afford to ignore environments whose demands they must satisfy if they expect to continue to receive required resources. Thompson and McEwen point out that only rarely have organizations been able to so dominate their environments that they could set goals and carry on activities without considering the reactions of those outside the organization.[6] They cite the *zaibatsu* corporations in Japan and the old Standard Oil Company in the United States as examples of these unusual autonomous organizations. Certainly publicly supported organizations such as SEAs are not in such favored positions.

At the same time, most organizations cannot afford to be so open to environmental influence that they risk loss of control over internal activities. Maintaining a balance between cooperation with the environment and autonomy of organizational action is a difficult task, particularly in times of uncertainty.

To survive and grow, therefore, organizations seek to establish good relationships with the organizations they work with. As a first step they try to make order out of their environment, sorting out from among a vast array of organizations those that are relevant to their particular situation. In times of uncertainty this is a particularly complex process, but such are the times when the effort is most required. When previously stable relationships become tenuous, organizations must be sufficiently open and aggressive to negotiate changes in their environmental relations. As Katz and Kahn note, since the

> environment is subject to technological, legal, cultural, climatic, and many other kinds of change, the organization is characteristically confronted with demands that it change, too, in order to maintain its relationship with the environment or establish a new one on the terms now available. Thus a systematic state of environmental relationship which was optimal initially may become inefficient or completely unfeasible.[7]

In short, organizations *must* learn to adjust to their environments. As Thompson and McEwen conclude, "Whether the process of adjustment is awkward or nimble becomes important in determining the organization's degree of prosperity."[8]

Strategies of Influence

Intraorganizational controls that assure cooperation of system members toward goal attainment cannot easily be brought to bear upon *interorganizational* relations.[9] Internal bureaucratic features such as hierarchy of authority, rights of command, formal offices, clearly specified, formal lines of communications, and agreed-upon role differentiation are not available to system leaders for interorganizational relations. Organizational leaders who have to relate to other organizations must, thererefore, be able to devise and employ influencing strategies that transcend bureaucracy.

In the present discussion we shall employ the typology developed by Heskett, in which he notes five strategies that organizations use when attempting to influence other organizations: *reward, coercion, expertness, legitimacy,* and *identification.*[10] *Reward* as a strategy is used by an organization when it is able to convince other organizations that they will benefit by cooperating in an endeavor. Rewards range from the extrinsic, such as funds, to the intrinsic, such as verbal recognition. *Coercion,* the reverse of reward, is used by an organization when it is able to convince other organizations that they will suffer losses if they do not cooperate. Coercion can be limited to threats or be expanded to actually include punitive measures such as cancellation of lucrative contracts. *Expertness* is used by an organization that possesses, or at least is believed to possess, "special knowledge" required by other organizations to carry out their own ends. This strategy, which is the stock-in-trade of consultant firms, is also available to organizations that conduct research or have special access to information sources. *Legitimacy* can be employed by an organization that by law, contract, or some other formal agreement can oblige other organizations to accede to its demands. Finally, *identification* can be used by an organization if others view association with it as desirable or prestigious: the Harvard business school can more easily obtain industrial cooperation for case study sites than can the business school of a small state college.

The ability of an organization to employ these strategies depends upon several factors. First, it must believe there is a need to establish and maintain environmental relationships. This may appear obvious, but there is often a time lag between environmental changes and the recognition of these changes by organizations. For example, many SEAs were slow to recognize their need to establish relationships with the educational materials suppliers that have grown in importance since the establishment of recent federal programs.

Second, the availability of power bases varies. Some organizations possess more special knowledge than other organizations. Similarly, some organizations are considered to be more legitimate than other organizations. The issue is further complicated by the fact that some organizations are more susceptible to certain strategies than are other organizations. SEAs can use their own legitimacy to get school districts to abide with their demands, but legitimacy is not as effective when they deal with university centers.

Third, the effectiveness of these relationships will vary according to the preferences and skills of the organizational members who are charged with managing them. If they view this role as significant and they are adept at managing nonbureaucratic strategies, their organization will probably be able to balance the need to gain environmental cooperation with the need to maintain organizational autonomy. If they do not see the value of such efforts or they are not skilled in influencing others, then it is unlikely that their organization will be able to make the adjustments that are required and it will probably suffer loss of resources needed to accomplish its purposes.

A View of the SEAs and Their Organization-Sets

Figure 13, which combines an earlier visualization (Figure 6) with the interorganizational influencing strategies described by Heskett, stresses the reciprocal nature of relationships between SEAs and their organization-sets. The ability of the SEAs to establish and maintain preferred relationships depends on their own and their organization-sets' perception that the payoff is worth the effort, the frequency with which they use strategies available to them, and the skilled manpower available to manage interorganizational relations. It is also influenced by the unique attributes of each of the sets of organizations with which SEAs interact. What may be appropriate and/or effective with one set of organizations may not be appropriate and/or effective with another set of organizations.

Relevant environmental organizations can be grouped into three sets: those superior in the line of authority, those subordinate in the line of authority, and those outside the line of authority. Those organizations grouped as superior in the line of authority possess the right, based upon constitutional provision, statutory privilege, or regulatory oversight, to impose their policies and program preferences. Those organizations superior to SEAs are Congress, OE, and state legislatures and governors. Federal involvement justified on the basis of the "general welfare" clause of the Constitution (Article I, Section 8) has, over time, allowed Congress to establish laws and provide resources for educational programs that meet national objectives. SEAs are expected to manage these federal programs and to assure Congress that its intent will be served. In the process, SEA relationships with OE, their federal counterpart, have become increasingly important. At the state level are the relationships between SEAs and legislatures and governors' offices, which have been established for a longer period of time and are based on a clearer mandate to perform required duties. SEAs have been expressly established and maintained to oversee school district compliance with state constitutions as interpreted by legislatures and governors.

Organizations subordinate in the line of authority are accountable to SEAs for their actions. The school districts that operate educational programs, and the intermediate educational units that support them act as delegated agents of the state and report to the SEAs, which oversee their activities on behalf of state legislatures and

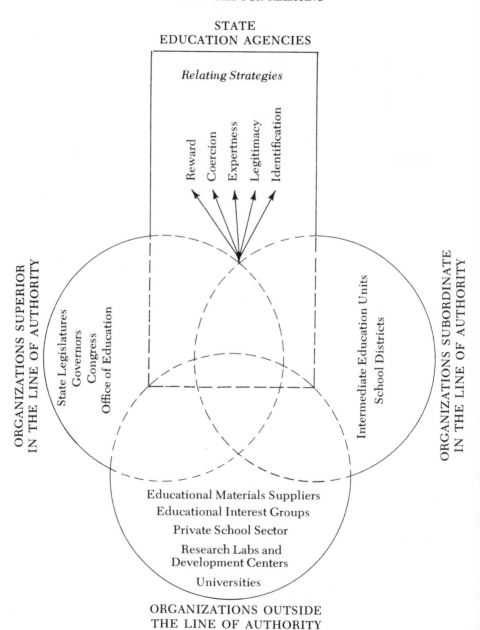

FIGURE 13. SEAS AND THEIR ORGANIZATION-SETS:
STRATEGIES FOR RELATING

governors. The recently expanded intervention of the federal government has broadened the SEAs' regulatory role and has provided additional resources for such efforts. As a result SEAs have found themselves involved in more frequent interactions with subordinate organizations.

The last organization-set, those organizations that lie outside the line of authority, presents SEAs with their greatest challenge. There are no established mechanisms to guide these interorganizational relations. Whereas those organizations that are superior or subordinate can be approached within the context of a relatively clear set of constitutional provisions, laws, and regulations, there are no such readily available guidelines for relating to organizations outside the line of authority. They have few if any rights to make demands upon SEAs; nor are they required to cooperate with them. Not constrained by membership in a formal intergovernmental authority structure, they choose to relate to SEAs only if they are convinced that SEAs possess rewards or expertness or they identify with these state agencies. Relationships with these outside organizations are also affected by precedents. Educational interest groups have traditionally maintained close ties with SEAs in their attempts to influence state-level policy-making in education. However, educational materials suppliers, who try to capitalize on the availability of federal resources to develop and market educational programs and equipment, have never related more than superficially with the SEAs. Thus, while the SEAs can rely upon rather clear and long-established patterns of interaction with educational interest groups, they must create entirely new strategies if they hope to regulate the activities of the suppliers.

We shall now explore the impact that has been generated by the establishment of the NDEA and ESEA on relationships between the SEAs and their organization-sets. In turn, we will review the activities of SEAs in dealing with organizations subordinate in the line of authority, organizations superior in the line of authority and, finally, organizations outside the line of authority.

Organizations Subordinate in the Line of Authority

"The constitutional power of state government has been in constant tension with a widely held value that the soundest educational policy is derived locally." This value has led state legislatures to delegate responsibility for the operation of schools to school districts.

The exceptions are in Hawaii where there is a single state school system and thus there is "no such delegation of authority, and a few states, especially Alaska and Maine [which] administer some remote rural schools directly from their state departments of education."[11] Local control of education as a concept was not widely challenged as long as the SEAs' role was limited to distributing state funds and auditing local school district records. In recent years, with increasing state fiscal input and, in particular, with the advent of federal programs, the need for the SEAs to intervene in the affairs of subordinate organizations has increased dramatically. As a result, the SEAs have had to consider the effectiveness of their traditionally nonauthoritarian relationships with school districts and intermediate educational units.

School Districts

State education aid, for the most part, is granted to meet general school purposes that require only a minimum of SEA supervision so there is no pressing need for extensive state-local interactions. However, relations between school districts and SEAs have increased markedly as a result of federal-program input. Now, school district officials must deal with SEA administrators when applying for federal funds and, often, are required to submit program proposals for review and approval by their SEAs.

Traditionally SEA officials have maintained collegial, nonthreatening relationships with school district officials. A policy statement distributed by the California SEA is fairly representative: "the administrative function of the Department is performed . . . by the Superintendent and his staff through professional direction and leadership rather than by direct intervention in local school administration and by professional advisory and consultant services to local school personnel."[12]

It has been difficult for most SEA leaders to demand that school district administrators meet the intent of categorical programs, a difficulty due largely to their professional ethos and the absence in the past of any real urgency to make such demands. In many instances, SEA administrators have attempted to implement federal programs within the context of established SEA–school-district relationships. Many SEAs have developed only minimal structures and made few decisions in the belief that school districts should be given maximum opportunity for self-direction. Wirt concludes that in New York the SEA sees its role as assisting local school boards to "accomplish their objectives, not to follow some state purpose. Local 'professionals'—or 'peers'—are thought to be the ones to make important decisions on local programs. Conflict with local school districts is carefully avoided and is considered evidence of failure to communicate."[13] In Massachusetts, Iannaccone has found that this practice, which is so prevelant that he has labeled it "The Religion of Localism," has restrained the SEA from playing an aggressive role.[14] This "religion" seems to be pervasive. One California SEA staff member responsible for NDEA Title III regulations stated: "I don't think we want to be a policing agency in terms of following up to see if people did what they said they were going to do. The key to our success is that most of the decision making is done at the district level. They know their abilities, needs and financial situation."

There are, of course, examples of SEA administrators who do not necessarily see their role as providing maximum opportunity for local-level self-direction. Wilson Riles, while directing the California ESEA Title I program, clearly viewed his task as the accomplishment of program ends, even if this meant putting pressure on school districts. He concluded:

> I've been around for eight years. What usually happens is that the district sends its budget man up. He is concerned only with how to get the dollars, not with methods or programs. He doesn't bother with that. If this is to be a program operation, we must have mechanisms to ensure that when they come for the money, we can nail them.[15]

The results obtained by school districts from federal programs are at least partially dependent on which approach prevails among those charged with program management in SEAs. If the conservative approach dominates, then program objectives may be modified or even sacrificed in favor of maintaining good relations with school districts. Soon after NDEA Title III became effective the California NDEA Bureau found that it was receiving more applications for matching equipment grants than there was money available. Instead of setting priorities at the state level as a basis for selecting preferred proposals, the bureau's response was to modify the state plan from the original stipulation that school districts would be funded "in the amount of one-half of the expenditures for approved projects," to read "in an amount up to one-half of the expenditures" for approved projects.[16] In other words, the bureau decided to give less to more school districts so that as many projects as possible could receive some minimal support, rather than establish rigorous state-level criteria for project selection.

A similar finding was made in Massachusetts by Iannaccone. In this state the SEA decided that ESEA Title II Funds "should be spread around." Iannaccone concludes that the SEA and its ESEA Title II Advisory Council were "more concerned with being fair to all the districts than in really carrying out the federal priority . . ."[17] The decisions by the California and Massachusetts SEAs may have preserved good relations, but probably at the cost of diluting "stimulation." When school districts realize that they will all receive funds, even if at a reduced level, there is little or no incentive to develop well-thought-out proposals. And, from the federal perspective, the chances that any effort will reach the critical mass necessary to evoke substantial change is radically diminished by the something-for-everyone dilution.

If the more aggressive approach dominates, as it did in the Office of Compensatory Education that administers ESEA Title I in California, then program objectives may be more fully attained but good relations with school districts may be jeopardized. The staff in the Office of Compensatory Education under Riles' leadership, identified more closely with the objectives of compensatory education for the disadvantaged than they did with relating to school district officials—"when they come for the money we can nail them." As Riles concluded, "my viewpoint is that this is not just money to help districts build buildings or buy projectors, it is to meet the needs of deprived children."[18] Given this philosophy, he encouraged his staff not only to urge school districts to meet the requirements set down by federal law and accompanying regulations and guidelines, but to press them to exceed these stipulations when there was evidence of such a need. The staff insisted on maximum concentration of resources on the deprived and limited efforts to identifiable target-area schools.

The California group also moved beyond federal intent by mandating the formation of school district Title I advisory bodies to be composed of parents from target-area schools. They even withheld funds already allocated when they felt that school district personnel could develop better program designs and more rigorous evaluation schemes. As might be expected, this kind of task orientation leads many school district officials to complain, as did one who responded to the survey: "It really seems like nearly everyone well detached from the local level—i.e., federal and state administrators—have decided that they are fully qualified to know what is best for the local schools and that change can be accomplished by fiat."

These examples indicate that SEA–school district relations should not be viewed as monolithic in nature. So long as there are categorical aid programs and SEAs retain specialized units to administer them, there will probably be varying approaches to such relationships, even within single SEAs. Therefore, while the dominant theme in SEA–school district relations appears to approximate the approach represented by the NDEA bureau, there will probably always be instances of the maverick approach represented by the Office of Compensatory Education.

Whether aggressive or conservative in their approach, most SEAs have relied on two basic strategies to help school districts operate federal programs. The first is to call upon school district personnel to lend assistance in establishing guidelines and to provide advice on SEA structures for managing the new resource inputs. For example, top-level school district administrators are sometimes brought to the state capital or gathered together at regional meetings to provide guidance for SEAs as they work out their management plans. These "think groups," or advisory committees, provide criticisms that can be considered *before* policies and practices are set. In New York, for example, Wirt found that advisory committees composed of key school district personnel have been most useful as a vehicle for overcoming resistance and generating support.[19] Of course, such committees also provide SEAs an opportunity to enhance professional ties with their school district colleagues. School district personnel are also employed by SEAs as program evaluators or curriculum consultants once programs are launched. This practice facilitates good rapport at the same time that it permits SEAs to employ skilled manpower on a short-term basis.

The second strategy is to reach out to lend assistance to school districts. This strategy can be employed at various points along a support-direction continuum. At the support end of the continuum, SEAs sponsor regional meetings to inform school district officials about new or amended federal programs, suggest ways that districts can best use their limited manpower resources to obtain program funds, and answer their questions. SEAs also disseminate results of exemplary school district programs to urge districts to consider program-design alternatives. Occasionally SEAs sponsor statewide meetings of program specialists to provide a forum for information exchange across school district boundaries. Midway along the continuum, SEAs sponsor in-service workshops to provide needed training for school district personnel. For example, ESEA Title II administrative funds are often used by SEAs to develop and run in-service workshops for school district librarians. Some even help districts evaluate their own activities through SEA-staffed review services.

At the direction end of the continuum, SEAs can require school districts to do certain things such as meet specified deadlines, account for expenditures, and include parent participation in planning for programs. Sometimes this practice works to the advantage of school district administrators. That is, SEAs can "run interference" for school district officials who want to implement controversial concepts, but are confronted by significant opposition at the local level. For example, school superintendents who want to establish compensatory education programs often find that middle-class school boards are reluctant to support them. When their SEAs take a firm stand on ESEA Title I requirements such administrators can shift the displeasure of their boards to the SEAs. That is, they can implement what they believe to be right without incurring the wrath of their school boards. One school district administrator in California told the state's ESEA Title I director that the SEA's demand for compliance with federal and state requirements was most useful: "By requiring us to do these things, we were able to do something we knew we should have been doing but we feared to do politically."[20] Of course, such directive behavior by SEAs is not appreciated by school district officials if their ideas differ radically from those of their state-level counterparts. When such is the case conflicts are likely to occur and district officials will often attempt to modify SEA intransigencies any way they can, including taking recourse in the courts and petitioning legislators to intervene on their district's behalf.

The SEAs' ability to reach out to lend assistance to school districts is highly dependent upon several factors. For a start, how they choose to organize and deploy their limited manpower resources is crucial. If SEA administrators remain desk-bound at the state capital it is not likely that they can be of much help to school districts. Many school district officials report that SEA administrators rarely make on-site visits and that, in many instances, the names of SEA co-ordinators of federal programs are known to them only because they appear at the top of a steady stream of memos. Iannaccone's pointed comment regarding the Massachusetts SEA could well be made about many other SEAs: "Supervisors do not get into the field enough and cannot look much below . . . paper statements on program activities. Site visits are made, but not often and not for long."[21]

The SEAs' ability to reach out to the districts is also affected by the size of their staffs. Survey results yielded interesting and somewhat unexpected results regarding SEA staff size and school district relations. School district administrators in states with less than 250 SEA personnel were most positive about the effectiveness of SEA communications with school districts concerning the status of federal program proposals; 82% of this group agreed with the statement that the SEA does a good job in this area as compared to 69% of school district administrators in states with 500 or more personnel in the SEA. Though not a large variation, it is intriguing that the smallest SEAs, with fewer personnel available, are perceived as most effective in their communications with school districts while the largest SEAs, with many more personnel available, are viewed as least effective. Perhaps school district personnel are better able to comprehend and penetrate the smaller SEAs and get to know their personnel because of their limited staff size; whereas the larger SEAs, with their more complex divisions of labor, present formidable barriers to such relationships. It is also possible that, as SEA staffs increase in size, there is more need for internal communication and co-ordination, leaving less time for SEA officials to relate to school district officials.

Finally, SEA officials often find it especially difficult to establish relationships with large city school district officials.[22] Often these relationships are strained because of hesitancies on the part of SEA officials who have rural and suburban orientations. One SEA administrator from Connecticut candidly noted:

> There are occasions when urban school districts are prepared to engage the lay and professional community in coming to grips with root issues. These opportunities should induce the SEA to marshal federal and state support—funds and personnel—in an integrated fashion. It should *not* be the problem of the school district to deal with the many state and federal desks which could or should contribute to such an effort. The SEA and its federal counterparts should jog their bureaucracies to affect such integration. Active, aggressive assistance to urban centers should swiftly become an urgent SEA priority.

However, SEAs often encounter substantial resistance when they attempt to interact with large city administrators. In part this is due to the perceived lower status of these state-level administrators because they are usually paid far less than those in top urban school district positions. It is also due to the fact that large city school systems normally retain program specialists with more years of relevant urban experience than the rural oriented SEAs can possibly marshal. For example, in a recent survey focusing on urban school districts and SEAs, Watson found that of 15 possible reasons to contact SEA staff members, city school officials only sought out these state officials regarding the question of additional funding. He concluded that "the disdain of state departments, common to personnel in city school districts, was further exacerbated when SEA staffs with rural orientations attempted to advise sophisticated staffs in the cities."[23]

Intermediate Education Units

A majority of states maintain an education unit somewhere between the state and local levels. Thirty-two states have a three-level structure, whereas 17 have only state and local structures, and one, Hawaii, has a unified state system.[24] Normally the intermediate role is played by county government, but such units can also be specially devised to meet regional educational needs that transcend county boundaries, as do New York's Boards of Cooperative Educational Services. However they are organized, results of the case studies in California and New York indicate that intermediate education units seek to perform duties beyond those minimally required by the SEAs in connection with federal categorical aid programs. Often this is because they feel there are advantages to be gained if they expand their realms of responsibility.

In California the county education agencies have been confronted with mounting criticism, centering around the belief that there are too many of these units—54 in total—given their limited role in educational governance. In fact, a formal report prepared in 1964 for the SEA by an outside consultant firm specifically recommended that the number of intermediate units be drastically reduced.[25] Furthermore almost annually one or more legislators interested in economy in government services sponsors a measure to reorganize the intermediate education structure in California.

Many county education offices have actively sought to increase the importance of their roles in an attempt to convince the SEA and the state legislature that they should not be reduced in number or size of staff. In 1960, at the California SEA's suggestion, Lake County in rural northern California began to write combined NDEA Title III project requests for the many small school districts within its jurisdiction. Many of these school districts would not otherwise have been able to participate in the program because they did not possess sufficient technical skills to develop their own project requests. The concept worked well and within a year most California county education offices copied the Lake County example. California's education code authorizes such activities, stipulating that county education offices should "provide professional and financial assistance to school districts which otherwise, because of size or location, would not be able to furnish a satisfactory program of education for their children." Still, the swift response of county education offices to this need indicates a pervasive desire to serve, or at least to be *perceived* as desiring to serve.

The county units in California are also called upon to help with other federal programs. The Office of Compensatory Education, for example, uses them to supply information needed to establish aid formulas, host regional meetings, and distribute state and federal documents to school districts within their jurisdictions. These county offices receive no extra funds from the SEA to cover the cost of their services. SEA officials argue that the counties' regular support funds should cover the cost of providing these services. The county offices rarely complain, however, because they realize that, in order to counteract the criticisms that they are inefficient operating units, they must demonstrate a capability to provide important services for the SEA and school districts.

The counties' need to serve can be a mixed blessing for SEAs. While the counties relieve the SEA of routine dissemination chores, they can also effectively restrain innovative approaches to solving the state's education problems. The California SEA was one of the first in the nation to propose that ESEA Title III supplementary centers be organized on a regional basis to promote innovation across district lines. In response the county education offices put pressure on the SEA and the state legislature to be given responsibility for and control of these centers. Once granted this authority they established consortiums of neighboring counties to manage the Title III centers. As might be expected, once given approval, the aggressive county offices did attempt to meet intended purposes, but others sought program control only to inhibit the dissemination of innovative practices.

In New York the Boards of Cooperative Educational Services (BOCES) are organized on a regional basis and are supported primarily through remuneration for contractual services provided for school districts in their jurisdiction.[26] Thus they prosper to the extent that they provide services deemed necessary and are not subject to the criticism lodged against their California counterparts of being superfluous. Yet the phenomenon observed in California of intermediate units aggressively seeking to establish a major role in the management of federal aid is also observable in New York. The BOCES have attempted to obtain a predominant position in the supervision of New York's ESEA Title III regional centers in much the same manner as have the counties in California. The BOCES's lobbying activities to gain jurisdiction over the regional centers have met with mixed success; in some cases they actually merged with the centers. One OE administrator familiar with New York's Title III activities concluded that "perpetuating the BOCES really became one of the main objectives rather than the promotion of educational change." In this instance, however, as Wirt has noted, the BOCES "did not monopolize the funds . . . because the program's sponsors feared BOCES would be dominated by traditionalists, while new ideas were needed."[27]

Strategies of Influence

As they relate to subordinate organizations SEAs are in a good position to employ the five bases of power.[28] *Reward* strategies include granting recognition to school district administrators by calling upon them for advice in the implementation of new or amended federal programs; standing behind district administrators who want to establish controversial federal programs; and providing expanded functions for the intermediate units that support the case for their continued existence and growth. School districts and intermediate units, in turn, reward SEAs by achieving intended outcomes.

Coercion strategies are pursued most often by SEA program administrators who are program-oriented rather than district-oriented. Such strategies include the withholding of program funds if federal intent is not fully met and, sometimes, by establishing state-level rules that are more specific and demanding than federal requirements. SEAs can also insist that intermediate units use their

own resources to meet program needs. On the other hand, intermediate units and school districts can coerce SEAs into expanding
their functions by complying minimally or by lobbying at the state
capitol.

Expertness can be a potent SEA strategy. Once briefed by OE,
SEAs can send well-known SEA professionals to regional meetings
throughout the state to share their knowledge of federal program
objectives and to explore the feasibility of alternative program designs with school district personnel. With direct access to OE information sources, SEA staff members, more than ever before, have
come to be viewed by subordinate organization officials as knowledgeable professionals. This image is enhanced as a result of the
SEA practice of defusing potential conflict situations by passing key
decisions on to the school district level. This expert image becomes
somewhat tarnished, however, when SEA officials work with large
city school district administrators who view themselves as more
knowledgeable than their SEA counterparts.

Legitimacy clearly works to the advantage of SEAs. School districts and intermediate education units, as agents of the state, are
answerable, through the SEAs, to the legislature and governor for
their actions. Furthermore, federal programs usually explicitly require that school district proposals be approved by SEAs before
they are eligible for funding.

Finally, *identification* as a strategy of influence has been extended by the introduction of federal aid. There are now more opportunities for SEA staff to demonstrate their preference for professional, collegial relations with school district and intermediate
education-unit personnel. Such subordinate organization personnel
can also be extensively employed as consultants and evaluators.
These practices have expanded identification by bringing subordinate organization professionals into the SEA network. In fact, many
of these personnel have come to view the SEAs as a good place to
work; as SEAs expand, recruits are often selected from among
school-district and intermediate-unit administrators. Of course,
identification can work in both directions; as the SEAs become more
identified with subordinate organizations, opportunities for school
districts and intermediate units to influence the SEAs increase. In
addition, there are two important exceptions to the SEAs' ability to
employ identification as a power base. First, as noted, SEA officials
are at a disadvantage in relating to large city school-district officials
who do not view such relations as particularly prestigious. Second,

when federal program co-ordinators in SEAs are more program-oriented than district-oriented, relations tend to be marked by friction rather than camaraderie.

Organizations Superior in the Line of Authority

At the other end of the authority continuum there are four organization-set members that are able to impose their will upon SEAs: state legislatures, governors' offices, Congress, and OE. SEA officials are required to develop ways to deal with all four organizations because they initiate demands and provide resources. How well the SEAs fare in these relationships significantly affects their ability to provide leadership for education.

State Legislatures

Legislatures maintain public education in accordance with state constitutional provisions and state governors execute legislative policies. Berke and Kirst have concluded that, "at present governors and legislatures are unaware of the vast discretion they have."[29] While this is still true in many states, there are indications that a shift is occurring; as will be noted below, some governors and state legislatures are coming to realize their ability to influence the fate of federally funded programs. The probability is that this realization will lead to even more incursions into the SEAs' administration of federal programs by legislatures and governors in the near future.

During the 1960s, 23 states actually outpaced the resource input increases provided by the local level for education. In fact, by 1970 the average state share of support stood at a quite respectable 41.1%.[30] Trends indicate that full state assumption of funding for the public schools may become a reality in the future.

It would seem that state legislatures might welcome increased resources from the federal level, especially given the growing demand for state support of public education and the fact that revenue sources are less than stable. However, while most state legislators agree that state resources are severely limited and that the federal government ought to assume a greater share of support for functions such as education, many feel that there are substantial disadvantages involved when states accept federal resources. Legislators are concerned that the categorical programs to which these resources are attached will restrict the states' role in educational governance.

They have two major concerns: one, that federal and state preferences often differ; and, two, that, because SEAs receive a large portion of their budget needs from federal program sources, these agencies can circumvent legislative oversight and control.

FEDERAL AND STATE PREFERENCES. Because federal preferences, of necessity, are national in scope, the extent to which they meet the needs of each of the 50 states varies greatly: what is right for Georgia is not necessarily right for Massachusetts. State legislators, understandably, prefer to see federal resources come to the states as general aid.

Recently state legislatures have shown great interest in emulating the federal government's categorical aid example. State legislators have their own ideas about how best to achieve given purposes and, with growing frequency, to establish programs with greater specificity and more rigorous regulations than those of the federal government. As an example, the California legislature established a state-supported reading program in 1965, the same year that ESEA became law. The state's categorical program is highly specific, concentrating on the prevention and correction of reading disabilities in grades one through three. The legislation requires that participating school districts develop innovative and detailed program designs and evaluation schemes and provide a percentage of the funds from the local level to support their programs. However, school districts could more easily get ESEA Title I resources, free of matching requirements and without extensive design or evaluation schemes, to serve the same purposes. Not surprisingly, two years later only 4% of California's school districts had instituted the state's reading program. It was not until several years later that the state program grew to the level anticipated by its framers. A legislative fact-finding committee came to the conclusion that, while the objective should be "to provide the best educational benefit to the children in the classroom . . . many school officials readily admit their staffs plan program applications to meet the criteria of the agency which has the simplest application form or has the most funds to disburse."[31]

LEGISLATIVE OVERSIGHT AND CONTROL. To meet their preferences, state legislatures require SEAs to carry out requisite tasks. One way of securing SEA compliance is through approval or disapproval of operating budget requests. As long as legislatures remained the sole source of funds for SEA administrative support, this strategy was most potent. Now, however, the federal government has provided SEAs with a major alternative source of funds for administrative purposes. On the average, the federal government contributes over 40% of SEA expenditures for salaries, contracted services, equipment, and other expenses.[32] With an external input of this size, state legislatures can no longer always rely on SEA cooperation and so are increasingly turning to other ways of dealing with intransigent or unresponsive SEAs. Some mechanisms they have developed follow.

Hearings. Legislative committees, including those for education, hold hearings, which may be open to the public but more often are held in closed session, to elicit information and opinions before proposing action for consideration by the full legislature. Education committees have the right to call upon SEA officials to testify about their program activities, including the administration of federally funded programs. Even if they are not asked to present verbal testimony, SEA officials are frequently required to provide legislators with confidential information and special reports. SEA testimony and reports keep legislators current about agency directions. They also provide data upon which to base judgments of proposed SEA operating budgets.

In-house research. Some legislatures have established their own research staffs to develop independent information concerning state agencies, including SEAs, in an attempt to become free of "filtered" agency reports. As a result SEAs in these states no longer have a monopoly on data needed to devise legislation.[33]

Appointments. State legislatures can influence SEAs as a result of the role they play in the confirmation process for state boards of education and chief state school officers. In the 32 states with appointed boards, the governors are charged with this responsibility;[34] however, despite this fact, research indicates that state board members view legislators as more influential in the selection process than are governors' aides and advisors.[35] In 26 states, the state board is responsible for the selection of the state superintendent[36] and it is a reasonable assumption that they consider perspective candidates in light of their acceptability to the state legislatures. Finally, it is within a state legislature's power to appoint advisory committees or commissions to executive agencies if it so desires.

Budgetary controls. It is within the power of state legislatures to modify or deny SEA requests for additional funds, staff, and space. Such power can be used to restrain SEA requests for funds for federal program administration as well as for state program administration. Legislatures can deny SEA requests to increase their staffs or to have staff slots originally funded through federal support become permanent state-supported positions. Finally, as state agencies take on new projects they often require more working area, but state legislatures are hesitant to invest in additional space to house ever-larger bureaucracies, especially when such space is for programs they think may compete with state programs or may be short-lived or inappropriate. Thus SEAs frequently find they must absorb considerable numbers of new staff into already over-taxed physical structures or rent temporary quarters, often at great distances from the parent organization and insufficient for program needs. Such physical separations also increase the potential that these federal programs will not be well co-ordinated or integrated with other SEA activities.

Legislating administrative ground rules. There is some evidence that state legislatures intend to become major initiators of education policy,[37] a tendency noted in states as different as New York, New Mexico and California.[38] Legislatures that had formerly limited themselves to the establishment of state-aid levels are now beginning to specify educational categorical aid programs. It is also within their power to mandate administrative and programmatic parameters if they are dissatisfied with the performance of state agencies. In California the legislature constrained the SEA—which was then led by a highly controversial superintendent, Max Rafferty—by establishing centralized decision-making for education, including federal aid, within the legislature itself. As Kirst observes, "The legislative initiative in federal aid has been extensive and almost always in a direction opposed by the CSDE. Indeed, much of the legislation was designed to erode the state superintendent's influence over the administration of federal aid."[39] As a result, when the ESEA was established, the legislature devised administrative ground rules that had to be followed by the SEA. For Title I the structure of the administrative unit was written into law and the superintendent's right to appoint staff was severely curtailed. He was permitted to nominate candidates for the director's post, but he could not actually select this person. For Title III, the legislature moved to specify priorities and devise guidelines. In addition an advisory committee was established to oversee SEA activities and report to the legislature.

Furthermore, the legislature mandates program requirements when it wishes. For example, it required that resources targeted to the school districts under Title V be reserved for a few districts to test the state's proposed planning, programming, and budgeting system. Such legislative initiative also occurs in other states. In New York, for example, Wirt found that "Legislators have expressed increased interest in the NYSDE administration of Federal Funds . . . as a direct result of *unresponsiveness* by those in charge of these programs to initiatives from legislative leadership."[40]

With this often used array of strategies at the disposal of state legislatures it is not surprising that SEA staff members view these bodies rather negatively. In fact, less than 40% of responding SEA administrators felt that their state legislatures facilitated their efforts to provide planning and leadership. One SEA official from Idaho thought that "it is impossible to understand why the SEAs fall short of expectations unless the legislature's ability to restrict SEA behavior is taken into account." An SEA administrator from Rhode Island commented that "SEAs should be allowed to use administrative funds as needed rather than be held to state rules about expenditure of these funds."

SEAs do have some leverage to modify the impact of these legislative incursions. They can use their legal governing bodies, the state boards of education, as protective shields. As a result of a major study of educational politics in the Northeast, Bailey, *et al.*, concluded that state boards "are less independent forces in their own right than [they are] sympathetic responders to the executive and administrative officials they oversee."[41] However, there are limitations to this strategy; as Mazzoni notes, state boards are often viewed by state legislators as political novices who do not consider the ramifications of their own policy preferences.[42] This view exists even in states such as New York where the Board of Regents is generally perceived to be a highly prestigious body. Futhermore, when these boards are appointed by governors there is the possibility that members are selected *because* they oppose SEA policies. This occurred in California in the early 1960s when Governor Pat Brown, a liberal Democrat, appointed board members who were in opposition to the policies of the politically and pedagogically conservative (and Republican) superintendent, Max Rafferty.

SEAs can work to counteract legislative pressures by effectively co-ordinating internal program activities. That is, it is less likely that legislatures will single out individual programs for attention if they are integrated throughout the overall structure of SEAs. Once programs are interwoven in the SEAs' substantial bureaucratic structures it becomes more difficult for legislators to clearly identify and modify specific programs. Occasionally SEA leaders are constrained from establishing such administrative patterns because of legislative interference, but most frequently their greatest problem lies with their own staffs. Administrators of individual programs perceive that recognition and advancement are based on visible and individual accomplishment so they tend to resist efforts to co-ordinate and integrate program activities. Only if the SEAs can overcome these professional preferences will they present a united and integrated structure that can mitigate against legislative incursions.

Finally, SEAs have historically been viewed as one of the major spokesmen for their states' educational communities. So long as they, and in particular their state superintendent, are viewed as experts in educational matters, they can influence the legislatures' actions. They can, for example, work with study groups, testify before legislative committees, confer with individual legislators, and cooperate with educational interest-group leaders, in order to effect legislation. So long as SEAs were the primary source of knowledge, this strategy was effective. It runs counter, however, to the recent tendency to centralize educational decision-making within legislatures. Today the SEAs' knowledge-leverage is less potent because legislative bodies are moving to build their own information networks.

In summary, state legislatures have a relative advantage over SEAs. They can reward or coerce SEAs through control of the state treasury. They often can resist federal preferences and attempt to use federal resources to meet their own preferred needs, even to the extent of legislating SEA administrative and programmatic requirements. They can also develop their own capacity to understand the educational needs of the states so they become less dependent on SEA experts. In response SEAs must rely on their dwindling monopoly of expertise, seek to integrate programs within their own structures to provide protective camouflage, and hope state school boards will come to their support when needed.

Governors' Offices

Governors and their executive staffs are charged by state legislatures with the implementation of enacted policy measures. Authority delegated by legislatures or granted by state constitutions can be brought to bear by governors to assure that state agencies accomplish the intent of policy measures.

Governors' offices can be important sources of environmental relations for SEAs. Unfortunately, governors and SEAs often vary considerably in their perceptions when they deal with educational problems. SEA administrators responding to the survey were as neg-

ative about the governors' impact on their activity as they were
about the state legislatures' impact: only 38% felt that governors and
their staffs facilitated the SEAs' efforts to plan for education in the
states.

Governors often view SEA administration of federal programs
in much the same way as do legislators. That is, they welcome the
federal money, which sometimes is used to relieve state budgets, but
they do not want federal preferences to supersede state preferences.
In addition, they fear that state agencies such as SEAs might use
federal funds to gain freedom from gubernatorial oversight.

The governors' ability to control SEAs varies with the authority
vested in their offices. In some states the governor's office remains
relatively powerless, reflecting traditional American suspiciousness
of power centralized under one executive official. In other states,
governors' offices have acquired extensive powers, especially in this
century. Today, in many states, governors prepare executive budgets
and/or legislative programs, work closely with their party's leaders
during legislative sessions, and retain the right to veto bills and
sometimes even individual items within bills with which they differ. In these states, as Sharkansky notes, governors can employ potent leverage to assure that legislatures enact their policy preferences, even if these preferences are at odds with legislative
programs of state agencies.[43]

Furthermore, where governors appoint state boards of education, they can press their point of view at the very top of the SEA
structure, by appointing board members who reflect their positions.
In California, Governor Brown shaped the state board in a liberal
image during his tenure. Governor Reagan, following Brown, reversed this trend, re-establishing the board in a conservative image.
In addition, where governor-appointed boards select state superintendents it can be expected that both the policy board and top SEA
administrators will be sympathetic toward the governors' positions.

The governors' ability to control SEAs extends beyond their
influence with the legislatures and their powers of appointment.
They normally supervise the states' personnel boards, which have
frustrated SEA efforts to recruit qualified personnel. The boards'
rigid interpretations of civil service requirements and the limitations they impose on salary schedules have kept many potentially
interested and highly qualified recruits from accepting, or even
seeking, SEA employment. Governors can employ their influence
on the boards to grant or withhold exceptions for SEAs. Most often,

to keep these agencies in check or to avoid giving the impression of showing preferences among executive agencies, they permit or even urge personnel boards to turn down exceptional SEA requests.

Control over SEA budget requests is also a potent lever. Governors incorporate proposed state-agency operating-budget requests in their fiscal messages to state legislatures. There are extensive negotiations between governors' staffs and SEA officials who must satisfy the queries of the governors' chief fiscal officers before their agency budgets are approved. In addition, once legislatures approve budgets, governors and their fiscal officers must attempt to insure that funds are spent as intended. In California any state-agency disbursements, including transactions that involve federal resources, must be approved by the budget division.

Finally, an important control mechanism available to governors is their right to establish central planning offices that transcend specific agencies' activities. As Jennings has documented, proliferating state and federal categorical aid programs have tended to cut across traditional agency boundaries, requiring co-ordinated interagency action.[44] By 1974, almost all the states had established planning offices—25 were located within governors' offices[45]—to oversee the executive agencies' program activities, including their deployment of federal funds.

The SEAs' ability to resist interventions by governors is, to an extent, dependent upon the powers that accrue to particular governors' offices. If a governor's powers are severely limited, then the SEA can focus its energies on the state legislature. If not, it must influence both or suffer restraints on budget, staff, and program prerogatives. Basic strategies available to SEAs in relating to governors and their staffs are much the same as those available for relating to state legislatures. They can attempt to employ their state boards as protective shields but this strategy is severely limited, particularly in states where the governor appoints board members. They can seek to co-ordinate programs within their structures so that it is difficult for governors to single out and deal with any one particular program, but this strategy runs counter to the preferences of many SEA program administrators. Finally, they can seek to establish a posture of eminent expertise that must be relied upon if the state is to achieve its educational policies, but this posture is becoming ever more difficult to maintain as educational problems prove difficult to resolve and as alternative sources of information become available to both governors and legislatures.

In those states where governors' offices have accrued influence mechanisms and the incumbent governor chooses to employ them, the SEAs are at a disadvantage. When governors possess power, they can control SEA budget requests, influence state legislatures and state boards of education to do their bidding, and employ state personnel boards and finance agencies to keep SEAs in check. Where governors possess and use these powers, the SEAs' ability to resist is severely limited. Prosperity probably depends more upon finding modes of accommodation than in direct confrontation with the governors.

Congress

As the federal role in education has expanded the states have found that the actions of Congress are directly relevant to their own destinies. Governors, legislators, and SEA leaders realize that the federal government's expanding role impinges upon their educational policy-making discretion. In 1964 James Conant, former president of Harvard, called for the evolution of "nationwide" educational policies determined by *cooperation among the states,* as opposed to "national" educational policy *set at a higher governmental level.*[46] His concept was enthusiastically received by state leaders, leading to the establishment of the Education Commission of the States. The commission includes governors and legislators as well as educators. However, because it has not been sufficiently supported by the states and because it has been unable to agree on basic purposes due to the diversity of views represented among the member states, it has fallen far short of providing Conant's hoped for "nationwide" educational policies.[47]

Congress has little direct dealings with SEAs because regulation of education policies is left to OE. Still Congress remains vital to SEAs because it establishes programs that they will ultimately administer. Recently this has become quite important as Congress' interpretation of the federal government's role in education has shifted from short-term emergency support to continuing and specific purpose educational programs, such as the NDEA and the ESEA.

To comprehend the impact that congressional actions have on SEAs, note the extraordinary responses that these agencies have had to make to the ESEA. ESEA Title I attempted to require that funds be "targeted" to schools where there are large percentages of educationally deprived youth. This necessitates that SEAs collect data to ascertain which schools qualify and then exert influence over school districts to assure that funds are actually channeled to these schools. In addition, Title I calls for participation of community members, including target-area parent groups. Title II calls for library resources to be "loaned" to private schools. Most state constitutions specifically forbid use of public funds for private schools so there are no precedent relationships and the SEAs have been challenged to bring public and private school officials together to work out procedures to accomplish congressional intent. Title III, until 1968, bypassed the SEAs altogether, substituting direct school-district–OE relations to establish innovative educational centers. This challenged traditional SEA–school-district relations. Eventually the threat moved SEAs to petition Congress to amend this title so that it included a specific and funded role for the SEAs.

SEAs, and school districts, are also constrained by Congress' funding practices. Appropriations for federal programs frequently are not authorized until after school districts are well into the academic year; exact allotments are not determined until even later. When, as has recently been the case, Congress fails to renew program authorization and/or to enact appropriations, program management becomes even more tenuous. When this happens Congress passes "continuing resolutions" and fiscally conservative school districts that must live with month-by-month federal allocations press SEAs to get earlier funding determinations.

State agency officials, as the "men in the middle," can inform their states' congressmen of state and local preferences. In return, they should be able to gain some influences over the deliberations of Congress. SEA leaders can lobby Congress to pass programs or program amendments compatible with their own and the school districts' preferences. However, many SEAs have not even begun to move toward such activities; about two-thirds of the SEA-administrator respondents reported that their agencies *never even attempt* to influence congressional behavior. In the few instances where they have, there is some evidence that their influence can be substantial. For example, the SEAs, through their lobbying organization, the Council of Chief State School Officers, concluded that direct OE–school-district negotiations regarding ESEA Title III projects were an encroachment and a direct threat to traditional SEA–school-district authority relationships. The council lobbied Congress until, over OE resistance, it amended Title III to include a supervisory role for the SEAs. As Scribner notes, this "was a major step in the direction of reaffirming the historic role of the state in the educational system of the country."[48]

SEAs will need to have more direct inputs to help Congress develop priorities before the enactment of legislation or when amendments are being considered. Although this concept was not widely accepted in the past there are indications that it is becoming a recognized managerial function. For example, the New York SEA has assigned one of its top officials to establish and maintain a liaison with the state's congressional delegation and to appear before congressional committee hearings to make known the agency's point of view about anticipated legislation. SEA officials in New York believe that the liaison has led Congress to modify intended legislation in directions they favor. Similarly, ESEA Title I concepts such as advisory committees composed of parents from target-area schools, pioneered by the California SEA's Office of Compensatory Education, have found their way into ESEA Title I amendments.

In summary, Congress has the ability to move SEAs to comply with national policies. It can limit or expand the SEAs' role by mandating administrative procedures, and by approving or withholding funds. It can even bypass SEAs in the administration of programs. The SEAs, for their part, must rely on the intercession of their congressional delegations and on their own expert status to persuade Congress to adopt their program and management preferences in new or amended legislation.

The Office of Education

The last member of the organization-set superior in the line of authority is OE, the SEAs' counterpart at the federal level. Being responsible to Congress and the President* for the execution of laws, it must secure SEA and school district cooperation in pursuit of congressional intent. This has presented a significant challenge.

---

*The President's preferences and actions are relevant to SEAs. But because his impact is indirect—through OE—the role of the White House is not explored here. OE, however, must be responsive to the preferences of the President for the same reasons that SEAs must be responsive to those of state governors. As the nation's chief executive, he is charged with assuring Congress that its laws are carried out. OE serves as the President's regulatory agency so its ability to function effectively depends on its maintaining good relations with the White House. The President's legislative program, budgetary position, and managerial preferences can either facilitate or constrain OE activities.

In particular, OE must attempt to move less advanced SEAs to meet the intent of Congress without getting in the way of those that are more competent.

Like SEAs, OE has had to make an unprecedented response to fulfill its role in the expanding federal intervention in education. As Bailey and Mosher have documented, OE was forced to institute several major reorganizations in the 1960s.[49] In 1960 OE had about 950 staff members. By the end of fiscal year 1965, when the ESEA was passed and while these reorganizations were still in process, OE had grown to 2,355 staff members. Still, OE has found itself hard-pressed to keep up with the expanding administrative chores associated with recent aid programs. As of 1970:

> There were some thirty professionals working on all facets of Title I— technical assistance, accounting, program support—[but] there were only three area desk officers for the entire nation. The one dealing with Massachusetts had responsibility for twenty-three other states, the District of Columbia, Puerto Rico, and the Virgin Islands. In addition to his Title I responsibilities, he spent approximately two-thirds of his time working on other projects at the Bureau level having practically nothing to do with Title I. The desk officer had no assistants and spent a substantial part of his Title I time drafting replies to Congressional mail. He felt that he could use at least four assistants to provide adequate technical assistance to the states.[50]

During these hectic years of readjustment, OE has found it difficult to provide adequate guidance for SEAs and school districts. As a result, school district personnel complain that OE has not established effective communications. They feel that there is a serious lag between the time decisions are made and the time that necessary information is disseminated. Even worse, as one SEA official from Florida noted, in the years after passage of the ESEA, OE's decisions tended to "change daily and confusion reigned. Only after several years of trial and error the rules of the game are emerging."

OE is also constrained by the fact that it resides in the midst of a politically charged national capital. An SEA administrator from South Carolina concluded that "OE is under such constant harassment by congressmen and the White House that the staff cannot pursue a continuing policy." Congressional education committees review OE activities with great interest, sometimes to the point of encroaching on its discretionary administrative powers.

There is often little that OE can do to repulse school district and SEA attempts to obtain favored treatment or special dispensations when officials from these state and local agencies call upon their congressional delegations to intercede with OE on their behalf. Commissioner Keppel's inability to enforce his decision to withhold ESEA Title I funds from the Chicago school district when he felt that it had not complied with federal intent illlustrates the debilitating impact that political pressures can have on federal agencies.

Still, there are strategies available to OE to assure SEA compliance. It develops guidelines that specify program purposes and processes, giving it an opportunity to interpret congressional intent, or, as is sometimes claimed, to legislate by rule making. OE guidelines often specify educational programs that can and cannot be supported, even though Congress may not have intended this. It can be argued that this OE prerogative, as an SEA administrator from Colorado noted, can "change the purpose of legislation. The law itself should be the guidelines." This criticism is sometimes shared by congressmen who feel that OE's guidelines frequently "don't seem to have very much to do with the legislation we thought we were writing."[51] By providing information and testifying before congressional committees, OE officials can impress their views on Congress as that body deliberates proposed educational legislation. Their influence can be significant as illustrated by their ability to convince Congress that ESEA Title III should be administered directly between OE and school districts.

Finally, because OE and SEA administrators have many common interests and both agencies are staffed by professional educators, OE officials have a natural entry into the SEAs. There is some evidence that OE exploits this opportunity: as noted, 81% of the SEA administrators responding to the survey felt that OE personnel are helpful to them as they plan for federal programs. The fact that OE maintains a special unit, the Division of State Agency Cooperation, to lend assistance to SEAs, even to the extent of providing them with management review services on a voluntary basis, indicates that it recognizes the value of maintaining good relations. The good will that accrues from the provision of such services is bound to increase OE's influence with SEAs. But this influence carries with it a cost. Maintaining a "special" relationship may require OE to make "special" concessions. As Kirst has noted, "There is a reluctance to confront state/local colleagues with whom [OE administrators have] built up 'good working relationships' over the years, especially if these colleagues do not want to conform to federal priorities or changes."[52]

The SEAs can also use these ties to their advantage. When SEA officials call on OE staff for assistance there is opportunity to impress these federal officials with the SEAs' positions. For example, perhaps because OE personnel are often invited by New York's SEA to sit on panels that review school-district ESEA Title III proposals, OE has rarely rejected a New York state-approved Title III proposal. In addition, SEAs can win advantages by offering their assistance to OE. SEA staff are logical resource people for OE to call on when it must make critical program-related decisions; SEA officials make themselves available to assist OE as it develops guidelines and sit on OE review committees that set priorities among project proposals. SEAs also provide a resource base for the recruitment of personnel for key OE staff positions. For example, recently several OE deputy commissioners have been recruited from the California SEA while the New York SEA has provided a U.S. commissioner of education. Such staff exchanges develop ties of identification that can be tapped by the SEAs as well as by OE.

The SEAs can also use their state plans, which must be filed with the U.S. commissioner of education before states can participate in most federal programs, to establish administrative flexibility. The development of state plans, if approached with serious intent, should help SEAs give early thought to management difficulties and make necessary adjustments *before* they become real issues. Although most SEAs do not put sufficient effort into the drafting of plans to capitalize on this possibility, there are a few exceptions. In California, for example, the director of the NDEA Bureau viewed state-plan drafting as an important chore. The broadly drafted California plan has permitted the bureau to make decisions in "gray areas."

Most important, SEAs that have taken the initiative to establish state-level priorities for federal programs have found that they can influence OE to adopt successful innovations in amendments to subsequent guidelines. For example, the California SEA's Office of Compensatory Education very early decided to require that school district project applications for ESEA Title I provide for target-area parent-advisory committees and adequate concentration of resource effort.[53] These requirements have both since been adopted in OE guidelines. One OE official noted that from the start members of the Office of Compensatory Education "asked us for interpretations . . . before we had even thought them out." As a result, OE observed the California SEA's experience and called upon its administrators to help OE formulate national policy in these sensitive areas. Wirt has drawn a similar conclusion regarding New York, noting that its SEA has pioneered many administrative practices regarding federal aid programs.[54] Thus "compliance" with federal guildelines, when looked at more closely, can be viewed as leadership by example. For instance, the New York SEA developed the notion of ESEA Title II "special grants" for priority library areas. The concept has since been adopted in more than half of the SEAs.

Finally, if all else fails, SEAs can exert political pressure on OE through their congressional delegations. As noted, they did so when OE attempted to establish direct administrative supervision of school-districts' ESEA Title III programs. However, such OE-SEA confrontations are rare. SEAs more often rely on interlocking memberships and the professional orientations of both staffs to influence their federal counterpart. As Murphy has observed, "USOE influence comes mostly from the power of persuasion, and since it is presently almost totally reliant on the states for information about local programs, it is absolutely essential that USOE maintain cordial relations with the states. Under these bargaining conditions, the states are in a position to exact a price for their good will."[55] He further states that "USOE's long-suffering attitude and differential stance toward the states can be understood in part as adaptive behavior designed to achieve the greatest possible influence from a weak bargaining position."[56] In short, OE is constrained in its program monitoring efforts by Washington's political dynamics and by the key linking position of SEAs. Such constraints permit SEAs relatively wide latitude for discretionary behavior.

The dynamics of OE-SEA relations are complex. They are similar organizations; each serves as a regulatory body for policy makers at their particular level of government. Furthermore, OE-SEA memberships are relatively interchangeable. OE employs guidelines, access to testimony with Congress, and their professional links with SEA staff to move the state agencies to comply with their bidding. SEAs, in turn, also exploit professional relations, help OE shape its guidelines, involve OE personnel in SEA decision-making, provide a source of staff recruitment for the expanding functions OE serves, develop innovations that OE can adopt, and as a last resort, rely on their states' congressmen to put pressure on OE or pass legislation that favors SEA preferences.

Strategies of Influence

Though SEAs have many advantages over subordinate organizations, they are at a distinct disadvantage regarding superior organizations. To begin, superior organizations can employ *reward* to attain SEA compliance. Congress and state legislatures can enact measures that include important roles for the SEAs; governors can appoint state boards of education that support SEA preferences and can influence state personnel boards and finance agencies to assist SEAs in securing their unique personnel requirements and budgetary needs; and OE can support SEA administrative and programmatic innovations and provide expert assistance when required. On the other hand, the SEAs' ability to reward these superior organizations is quite limited.

This organization-set can also apply *coercion* simply by denying SEA requests. Legislation can be punitive; note, for example, the California legislature's restrictions on that state's SEA regarding administration of ESEA titles, or Congress' refusal to grant an administrative role to SEAs for ESEA Title III during the first several years of that program. Governors can see that rigid personnel practices are instituted and can slash SEA budget requests. OE can devise constraining guidelines and influence Congress to pass laws that restrict SEA flexibility. SEA coercive influence over these superior organizations is limited to lobbying of state legislators and congressmen.

Probably the most frequently employed SEA influence strategy, *expertness*, is less potent now than in the past. Congress, OE and many state legislatures and governors, have developed independent capacities to collect and interpret the information required to make educational decisions. Thus SEAs no longer have a monopoly of information. In addition, the inability of educators to provide "answers," especially those required to satisfy the nation's commitment to equal educational opportunity, has jolted policy makers out of the belief that education is best left to the educators. The enormity of educational deprivation, especially in the inner cities, has overwhelmed educators' ability to respond. As a result they now tend to be viewed by policy makers, rightly or wrongly, as less "expert" than in the past. Rather than being the source of answers and aid they are now often seen as the cause of the problem

Legitimacy inexorably ties this organization-set and SEAs together. SEAs are required to execute policies that state legislatures and Congress establish and governors and OE oversee. In return, these organizations provide the means for SEAs to meet their demands. SEAs can count on continuing resource inputs as long as policy makers make such demands. Using SEAs to regulate school district activities pursuant to the needs of state and federal programs is a well-established practice. It is not particularly amenable to modification, as witnessed by the short-lived bypassing of SEAs in the administration of ESEA Title III.

Finally, *identification* as a strategy is limited in practice to OE-SEA interactions. There is a modicum of identification between top SEA officials and some legislators and governors' offices, but for the most part members of these superior organizations view the SEAs as service agencies established and maintained to do their bidding and, as such, not within their realm of policy-making relationships. Congress has had few direct dealings with SEAs and feels no normative constraints on its actions. OE, however, is intertwined with SEAs through professional norms and exchanges of ideas and personnel. Because the flow of ideas and personnel goes back and forth between state capitals and Washington, both SEAs and OE can employ identification as a strategy when necessary.

Organizations Outside the Line of Authority

The third organization-set is composed of organizations outside the formal authority system. They may differ from each other in many ways, but they share one critical characteristic: they have few if any constitutional or statutory reasons to cooperate with SEAs. There have always been such organizations in the SEA environment, but the federal government's intervention in education expanded their numbers and increased SEAs' need to work with them.

These relationships with outside organizations are often tenuous and managing them requires substantial ingenuity on the part of SEA leaders. The present exploration is limited to SEA relations with five organizations that appear to be particularly relevant to SEAs as they administer federal programs: educational interest groups, private schools, higher education institutions, research labs and development centers, and educational materials suppliers. Emphasis will be placed on the reasons these organizations and SEAs work together and on the strategies both use to attain desired outcomes.

Educational Interest Groups

SEAs and the interest groups representing school boards, administrators, teachers, and lay bodies have long found cooperation mutually beneficial in their attempts to influence governors and legislatures. By cooperating they can pool their independently gathered information, share the burden of influencing legislators and governors, and use their contacts with the state's education community to establish "grass-roots" support for their policy preferences.

Interestingly, the cooperation between SEAs and interest groups that exists to influence state legislatures and governors has not been transferred to the dynamics of federal aid. Examination of the results of the case studies and the survey failed to uncover such relationships, cooperative or otherwise. The Berke and Kirst team also examined the role of interest groups in federal aid, particularly those with an urban orientation, and found little activity or impact in any of the six states included in their study.[57]

There appear to be several reasons for the absence of interest-group activity. The payoff may not have been worth the effort in the past because federal input was relatively minimal. Second, most state-level interest groups are affiliates of national organizations that monitor federal activities in education. These groups, which include the National School Boards Association and the National Education Association, represent their state affiliates on issues ranging from preferred forms of federal aid to the decentralization of OE. State-level groups, with limited staff and funds, have been content to leave influencing activity in the federal arena to their parent organizations. Third, the distribution formulas for federal aid leave little room for interest groups to influence OE or SEAs. ESEA Title I, for example, is determined to the county level on the basis of poverty indices, and NDEA Title III is distributed on a matching basis, the cost being shared by participating school districts and the federal government. Fourth, in many states educational interest groups are presently dissipating much of their energies on internecine warfare. Increasingly, militant teachers' organizations stand in opposition to school boards and administrators' organizations over economic benefits. Similarly urban educators seek special treatment by legislatures and governors to redress past inequities, even at the expense of suburban and rural school districts.

There are a few indications that interest groups may come to play a greater role in the dynamics of federal aid as local and state resources become less available. They have already sought to influence state legislatures when these bodies contemplate passage of measures that might affect federal programs such as ESEA Title III. As statewide urban educational interest groups form, such as the Big Five in New York (New York City, Yonkers, Buffalo, Rochester, and Syracuse), it is probable that they will try to influence the federal government, as well as state governments, to reserve resources for city school districts.

If and when state groups do become involved in the debate over federal aid, SEAs will have to find ways to help co-ordinate their activities so that a united position can be presented before federal policy-makers. In New York, where this need has been anticipated, the SEA has called interest groups together to establish a joint SEA–interest-group position of support for educational appropriations by the federal government. As a result, interest-group leaders have joined with the SEA commissioner in testimony before Congress. This rare effort indicates that SEAs can work with educational interest groups if they take the initiative.

Private Schools

There has been virtually no interaction between the SEAs and private schools. Once they are licensed by the state, private schools are normally left free to operate their programs with little, if any, state regulation. For the main part the absence of regularized interactions is because, in maintaining the separation of church and state, the states have refused to provide financial aid for private schools, most of which are Catholic. California's state constitution is representative of this position: "No public money shall ever be appropriated for the support of any sectarian or denominational school, or any school not under the exclusive control of the officers of the public schools . . ."[58] Until very recently, when it appeared that many private schools might have to send their pupils to the public schools because they could not afford to stay open, state legislatures have vigorously maintained such constitutional restrictions.

In the last several decades Congress has slowly moved to the position that all children, whether in public or private schools, should participate in federal programs if they are otherwise eligible. To overcome the states' restrictions, Congress has employed several strategies. NDEA Title III matching funds have been made available for loans to private schools to buy some types of equipment. This provision has not been widely used because funds are limited and the reporting requirements are extensive. Still, the loans, negotiated directly between OE and the private schools, did set a precedent that was later extended under the ESEA. Congress has provided full funding for the ESEA so no state money is involved.

Citing judicial precedents such as *Everson* vs. *Board of Education*,[59] Congress has adopted the "child benefit" theory, which holds that benefits accruing to students such as transportation, secular textbooks, and medical care, should be granted regardless of the type of school the student attends. Furthermore, ESEA and its subsequent regulations and guidelines require that school districts process proposals and retain administrative responsibility for private school programs. In addition, title to books and equipment is retained by school districts so, technically, they are only on "loan" to private schools.

Once Congress accepted the "child benefit" argument it was inevitable that private schools would participate in federal programs. With passage of the ESEA, the SEAs were, often for the first time, required to establish relations with private schools. ESEA Title I guidelines call for "participation of educationally deprived children enrolled in private schools who reside in project areas." ESEA Titles II and III include similar requirements. Most SEAs have responded by publishing state-level guidelines that call for school districts to cooperate with private schools.

In many instances, however, such cooperation has proven quite elusive. Partially this is due to the absence of precedents. Because SEAs and school districts had few formal relationships with private schools in the past, what might otherwise have been viewed as routine interorganizational decision-making became a major effort to adjust to a new situation. The SEAs, with no established routines to draw upon, issued somewhat ambiguous guidelines for school-district–private-school interactions. School districts, for their part, have often viewed their tasks in the effort as unnecessary and menial chores that, as they see it, are complicated by private school reticence to provide the information required to file reports to SEAs.

In the few instances that SEAs have responded more forcefully to the challenge, there is some evidence that it is possible to move school districts toward meaningful relations with private schools. For example, within the California SEA's Office of Compensatory Education, the Bureau of Community Services has been assigned responsibility to insure that educationally deprived children in private schools have opportunities to participate in ESEA Title I programs. In pursuit of this objective, the bureau has sponsored statewide, regional, and local meetings between public and private school officials to overcome initial hesitancies and resistance. In addition, the bureau has formulated stringent state-level guidelines that go beyond the law and OE guidelines. They require that school-district project applications show their intent to involve private school children. To make the point clear, applications have been returned when there is not sufficient evidence of provision for cooperation with private schools.

Perhaps as a result, California did not have test cases in its state courts that challenged the validity of private school participation in ESEA Title I, as did such states as New York and Pennsylvania. Once school districts in California found that the SEA intended to uphold its guidelines, information began to flow between private schools and the local and state education units. In fact the Catholic church, through its Sacramento diocese, soon established a liaison with the SEA, assigning several officers to monitor federal program developments and obtain more federal funds for Catholic schools.

For the most part though, since SEAs are not normally inclined to enforce regulations strictly, it would be surprising if they were to move vigorously into the uncertain, and what many believe to be a most ephemeral, realm of school-district–private-school relationships. In fact, most SEAs seem to act in such cases only when it's absolutely necessary. Iannaccone found that Massachusetts SEA officials felt that "if private school officials do not complain and if there is minimum compliance with federal legislation and regulations, it is just as well to let sleeping dogs lie."[60]

Higher Education Institutions

In most states the control structure for public higher education is independent of that for elementary and secondary education. SEAs rarely have permanent, well-established relations with colleges and universities, even though such links would be highly desirable. Except for schools of education, which must comply with SEA certification requirements, there are no formal entry points for SEAs to gain a hearing in institutions of higher education. Extending cooperative relations would make sense because the public schools prepare students for entrance to colleges and universities, which in turn provide teachers for the schools. However, as Usdan, Minar, and Hurwitz have documented, rather than cooperating with each other, SEAs and universities are often in direct and growing competition for limited state resources.[61]

Federal programs often overlap the functions of universities and elementary and secondary schools so SEAs could profit by focusing more attention on higher education relations. Federal aid for higher education, student assistance, programs for the disadvantaged, institutional support, and college personnel development, amounted to almost $1.7-billion by fiscal-year 1973.[62] Some of these funds have been channeled into the training of teachers and counsellors. For example, during the 1960s NDEA Title V, Part B, and NDEA Title VI, Part B, supported institutes for guidance counsellors and teachers of foreign languages and NDEA Title XI supported institutes for teachers of English, reading, history, geography, and disadvantaged youth, and for library personnel and educational media specialists. There was no formal provision for SEA input into these institutes other than the dissemination of related OE literature to school districts.

In part the ommission may have been due to concern in Washington with the shortcomings of the less able SEAs. But it also was due to the fact that most institute directors tried to attract a national group of participants, and resisted attempts to shape curriculum to meet the preferences of a single state. The result was that institutes were usually organized with little consultation by state or local educational leaders and the impact on the schools was minimal. A 1966 evaluation of NDEA history institutes concluded:

> Objectives of institutes visited were not designed on the basis of a thorough study of or an acquaintance with the needs and problems of teachers and schools. . . . Often institute directors and instructors had not worked closely with teachers before, and only a few had ever participated in or visited school courses and programs. The majority were rather vague about what happens in the schools and what the social studies curriculum is. It is not surprising, therefore, that there was a good deal of uncertainty about just what the institutes ought to be doing for teachers.[63]

What little influence SEAs have on universities and colleges is pursued informally. One of the most common practices seems to be for SEA staff to urge their university-based friends to work on statewide committees to help shape curriculum guides. Professors are also recruited, often with federal funds, as consultants to school districts. Finally, using ESEA Title V funds as a resource base, SEAs occasionally employ university specialists to help plan for their own internal management co-ordination. The obvious limitation of these strategies is that, while they may bring university people into the public school network, they do not directly increase

SEA influence on research or course work being conducted by higher education institutions.

Research Labs and Development Centers

Research and development in the United States is given rather low priority, constituting less than one-third of one percent of overall national expenditures for education.[64] Even this small input has only recently been recognized as necessary, particularly since the passage of ESEA Title IV. Section 4 of this title amended the Cooperative Research Act of 1954 to provide for "Construction of Regional Facilities for Research and Related Purposes." These facilities, or labs as they have come to be called, were designed to achieve an ambitious array of tasks: conduct research, provide facilities and equipment for research, train research personnel, translate research outcomes into practical materials for school districts, and disseminate innovations.

SEAs, ostensibly, also carry out educational research. However, in most SEAs, research is given low priority. SEAs find that qualified research personnel are hard to attract, especially because of the limitations placed on state employment. Furthermore, the pressing business of regulation normally takes precedence with the time of the few SEA staff members who have research capabilities. One California SEA official admitted that "while research is theoretically one of the functions of the department, there isn't much of it going on. A little competition from the regional labs might be a good thing." Thus what OE has specified as the research and development labs' function, provision of an opportunity for researchers and administrators to discuss innovative program designs, may appear to be predatory on an SEA function, but in reality it has not resulted in a major confrontation.

SEAs, with no formal links to the research labs and development centers, have been hopeful that lab directors will at least keep them informed. However, while the labs have developed relations with universities, especially through schools of education, they have been slow in making efforts to involve field-related personnel such as classroom teachers, intermediate education unit officials, or SEA officers. These practitioners are especially under-represented on the labs' boards of directors.

Cooperative lab-SEA relations would appear to be beneficial to both parties. The labs could enhance their own images and have a greater impact if they could get SEA officials to disseminate their ideas and materials to school districts. SEAs, for their part, could draw upon the findings of labs, especially since their own research activities are minimal, to extend their capacity to serve school districts.

Educational Materials Suppliers

Educational materials suppliers have provided motion-picture projectors, audio-tapes, and printed materials for school districts since the 1920s. Their role has expanded dramatically since the 1950s, when technological breakthroughs such as educational television, computerized instruction, information storage, retrieval and distribution systems, programmed instruction, teaching machines, microfilm, and language laboratories broadened and complicated the interactions of industry and school districts.

Federal programs have provided schoolmen with opportunities to experiment with these technological breakthroughs. For example, NDEA Title III encourages purchase of educational equipment to improve curricula; ESEA Title I programs often require use of elaborate technological resources; ESEA Title II emphasizes the purchase of library materials; and ESEA Title III has encouraged industry to develop systems approaches for use by supplementary education centers. As might be expected, the availability of these resources has encouraged industry to develop products for use in the schools. As Keppel has noted, "A billion dollars looking for a good, new way to be spent does not ordinarily turn the American businessman into a shrinking violet."[65] During the 1960s educational materials suppliers, who had previously limited their activity to the production of "hardware," or equipment, began to develop "software," or program concepts, so that they could sell total educational packages to school districts. These organizations have only rarely had the impact originally anticipated because the hardware-oriented businessmen and their new partners, educators brought in to develop software aspects of the packages, have often been at odds.

In addition, relationships between educational materials suppliers and school districts have been constrained because most teachers have not been properly trained to use the "software-hardware" packages.[66] As a result many schools have equipment bought with federal funds that is inappropriate for program needs or, worse still, is pertinent but left in a closet to gather dust because there are no staff members who have the inclination or expertise to operate it. Shortly after passage of the ESEA a congressional committee studied the situation and found that school districts sometimes invest in inadequate or inappropriate equipment and that there is little chance of "reconsideration of choices once they are made." The committee concluded that "it is imperative that educators maintain and safeguard their proper role as formulators of educational policy."[67]

The SEAs should be able to help provide the necessary safeguards since they monitor school district applications for federal programs and are responsible for auditing school district expenditures. After some prodding by OE, many SEAs have responded by developing "approved lists" for equipment purchases. Several have also required school districts to identify program objectives before they submit lists of equipment needs. There has even been interstate SEA cooperation. Employing ESEA Title V funds, New York, California, Delaware, Illinois, New Jersey, North Carolina, Pennsylvania, and Texas have cooperated to determine the role of state education departments in the selection and evaluation of educational materials and equipment.

Such activity is fundamentally reactive. It is limited to "policing" school-district purchasing practices. What is called for, in addition, is an aggressive effort on the part of SEAs to interact with educational materials suppliers as they anticipate needs and develop concepts and equipment. However, SEAs remain passive and "hope for the best." Even in the more aggressive SEAs there have been few attempts to establish such links with industry. For example, one top New York SEA official has concluded that industry should "develop support systems that would help improve the quality and effectiveness of education. This has not yet materialized." One reason that it has not materialized may well be that industry does not receive the benefit of SEA and school district officials' counsel.

Strategies of Influence

Several conclusions emerge from these explorations of SEA relationships with organizations outside the formal line of intergovernmental authority. Because there are no specified authority ties, relationships tend not to be clearly delineated. With few precedents SEA officials can turn to for guidance, relations are more often sporadic in nature. SEAs have not committed much of their limited funds or manpower to the effort, possibly because there are few demands by policy makers that they establish and maintain such relationships. There are probably opportunities for SEAs to extend their leadership image if they can only seize the initiative and establish more extensive relationships with members of this organization-set.

The extent to which influencing strategies appear in these relationships varies, but generally they are more limited than in SEA relations with subordinate and superior organization-sets. *Reward* is of limited use. Except with the private schools, which must cooperate to receive federal funds, the SEAs are given no formal role in overseeing these organizations' participation in federal programs. Higher education personnel can be approached through consultancies, but SEA influence on their parent institutions remains minimal. Educational interest groups have thus far concluded that there is little payoff in spending their energies on federal aid issues. Unless their perceptions change, there is little the SEAs can do to involve them in this governance area. Educational materials suppliers, probably rightly, do not seem to think that working with SEAs will affect the sale of their products to school districts. Finally, research labs and development centers and SEAs have not recognized the potential mutual rewards that can be gained through cooperative activities.

There is relatively little *coercion* evident. The only use of coercion appears to be limited to SEA guidelines regarding private school participation in federal programs and the development of eligibility lists for educational equipment. It seems that with no formal or superior position *vis-à-vis* these organizations, the SEAs have little chance to be coercive.

Expertness is a constant theme, but it is as available to these outside organizations as it is to the SEAs. Educational interest groups seek information from SEAs, but they also have their own information sources that the SEAs can tap. The expertness available to higher education institutions and research labs and development centers is far greater than that available to SEAs. Educational materials suppliers command the talents of top educational designers, and thus far at least, have not felt that closer ties with SEAs would improve their effectiveness. Private schools, with their own hierarchies, have only recently been tempted into the SEAs' orbit to gain information about federal aid requirements.

Legitimacy is probably the strategy least available to SEAs.

Federal law stipulates private school participation in some federal programs; a few states formally co-ordinate higher education and elementary and secondary education; and equipment for schools must meet state-mandated minimum requirements. But beyond these few instances there are no formal constitutional, statutory, or regulatory mandates for these organizations to cooperate with SEAs.

Neither do such organizations *identify* with SEAs in the management of federal aid. Educational interest groups and SEAs have developed patterns of cooperation, but this cooperation centers on influencing state officials, not federal officials. There is no precedent for identification with private school officials; on the contrary, the SEAs' long-established relations with public school officials tend to retard SEA–private-school interactions. When public and private school administrators are in conflict there is considerable temptation to favor public school administrators, who must be relied upon for continuing compliance. Except for education professors, university staff members have felt little compulsion to work with SEA officials. This is even more true of research lab and development center staffs and educational materials suppliers, neither of whom has sought out SEA officials for guidance in their efforts.

Summary of External Responses

We have focused on SEA relationships with several organization-sets as they have been affected by the introduction of federal programs, particularly the NDEA and the ESEA. Organizations that have the ability to facilitate or hinder SEAs in the accomplishment of their purposes were categorized within three organization-sets. Organizations superior in the line of authority, including state legislatures, governors offices, Congress, and OE, devise policies that SEAs must institute. School district and intermediate educational units, as organizations subordinate in the line of authority, are required to accept SEA supervision. Organizations outside the line of authority, such as educational interest groups, private schools, higher education institutions, research labs and development centers, and educational materials suppliers, have few if any constitutional or statutory reasons to work with SEAs.

The SEAs' relations with these three organization-sets have been viewed from a framework of strategies of influence (see Figure 13), which were categorized as:

> reward—benefits perceived to accrue if organizations relate to one another;

coercion—threats or punitive actions that can be effected if organizations do not work together;

expertness—"special knowledge" that can be tapped through these relationships;

legitimacy—laws or other formal agreements such as contracts that require relationships between organizations; and

identification—associations that are prestigious or desirable.

Figure 14 depicts a rough estimation of the influencing strategies that were found to exist between SEAs and each of the three organization-sets, according to the balance, or lack of balance, of the influence between them; and the extent to which these influencing strategies seem to be employed.

Two conclusions are strikingly apparent. First, SEAs are more extensively involved with the organization-sets that are superior and subordinate in the line of authority than they are with the organization-set that is outside the line of authority. Second, the balance of influence varies greatly depending upon the particular organization-set. With the possible exception of large city school districts, SEAs have a clear advantage in their relationships with subordinate organizations. There is only one strategy that appears to benefit both sides equally—the feeling of identification between SEA and school district officials. Influencing relationships are reversed as regards superior organizations. Only expertness seems to be to the SEAs' advantage and even this is rapidly being eroded as policy-making bodies and executive agencies develop their own knowledge sources. There is an approximate parity in the relationship between SEAs and the organization-set outside the line of authority. However, this parity is due more to an *absence* of interaction than to any demonstrated equality between the two parties. The present power vacuum may well indicate that neither SEA leaders nor leaders of these organizations are convinced of the value of developing a relationship.

Organization leaders have to look beyond the confines of their own structures as they attempt to modify demands so that they are manageable. They must also obtain resources and move other organizations to cooperate in satisfying these demands. SEAs will have to overcome their inability to influence non-subordinate organizations if they are to fulfill their role expectations. Unfortunately, it does not appear that this will happen. Organizations outside the line of authority have yet to be convinced that there is advantage to be gained by extending relations with SEAs, while those organizations that are superior in authority are increasing their demands upon SEAs, as

FIGURE 14.   SEAS AND THREE ORGANIZATION-SETS: EXTENT AND
BALANCE OF INFLUENCE EMPLOYED

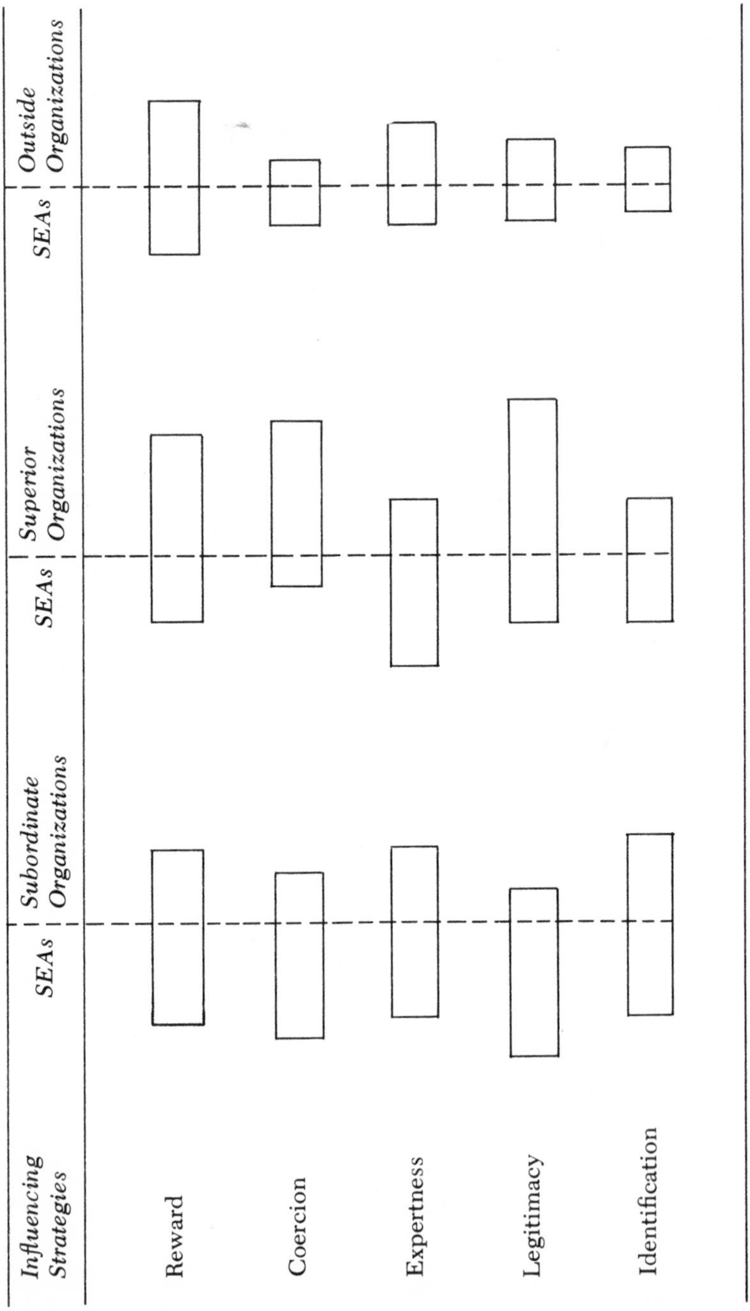

shown by the expanding number of state and federal categorical programs being funneled through the SEAs. Furthermore, these policy-making organizations are actively developing internal information systems that free them of their dependence on SEAs for data. In addition, there is an increasing tendency on the part of state legislatures to dictate SEA administrative arrangements.

SEAs do not seem to have fully grasped the significance of the situation. Their unresponsiveness may well be due to a preoccupation with sharp increases in SEA staff and internal reorganizations that have been required because of their expanded responsibilities in recent years. For whatever reasons, however, lack of SEA responsiveness to a changing environment has seriously impaired their ability to act independently. Encroachment on their activities by outside organizations can rapidly relegate SEAs to a minor and purely regulatory role in the intergovernmental control of education.

VI/SEAs As Responsive Organizations

Resources from the federal government account for about seven percent of total fiscal inputs for the nation's elementary and secondary schools. This is a relatively small share of total costs, but federal aid can be "the tail that wags the dog." Most state and local fiscal resources are fully committed to the maintenance of existing efforts, but the federal government, free of such constraints, can attempt to pinpoint its resource inputs on the margins of change. Its impact can be far greater than its proportional share of fiscal inputs would indicate. One immediate outcome is that SEAs have been challenged to move beyond the monitoring of state aid formulas to the management of major education programs. These adjustments are vitally important if the SEAs are ever going to become educational leaders and agents of change instead of the tradition-bound, highly bureaucratic, regulatory agencies they tend to be today.

Before 1958, federal programs channeled through SEAs affected only one aspect of their activities, vocational education. A decade later federal funds accounted for 41% of all SEA expenditures and covered the spectrum of educational programs. In fact, most SEAs have more than doubled their staffs and operating budgets since federal programs such as the NDEA and the ESEA were initiated. Although federal inputs leveled off in the early 1970s, the responses required to firmly establish the programs previously initiated still cause major disruptions in most SEAs. It took time for SEAs to become familiar with federal procedures and to discover the means to harness the resources provided. This was a difficult era for the SEAs, many of which were small and placid prior to the federal initiative and thus were challenged to upgrade their abilities.

Given the continuing ferment, it is difficult to determine

whether SEAs have the ability or the desire to enhance their capacity to provide educational leadership by responding effectively to the challenges posed by federal aid. But there is a sufficient backlog of experience that enables us to identify the most important problems they encounter and the general nature of their response. To summarize the discussion in the book and develop implications it may be useful to return to the frameworks introduced in Chapter II.

SEAs and Policy Making

The establishment of policies has been viewed as consisting of several consecutive stages. A period of *dissatisfaction* sets in as groups coalesce around "repressive" policies or the absence of desired policies. Over time, *attitudes crystallize* as group identity grows, grievances become relatively clear and leaders emerge to articulate the groups' causes. As *ideas are formulated,* dissatisfactions are translated into alternatives to the status quo and, assuming that *debate* can be widened, these alternatives are publicized, modified as required, and suggested as *legislation* to policy-making bodies by representatives of the dissatisfied groups. Finally, *implementation* completes the cycle as the few proposals that survive this hazardous process are assigned to agencies that function to assure compliance with the intent of rules and laws. Executive agencies such as SEAs often attempt to enter the process long before policy initiation. Many SEAs take an active interest in proposals that are put before state legislatures and some even develop their own policy platforms.

Interestingly, very few have shown an inclination to take such initiatives regarding federal policy-making for education. A notable exception was when SEAs, after earlier being bypassed in the administration of ESEA Title III, made a concerted effort to establish a role for themselves in this federal program. Congress amended Title III according to SEA preferences, indicating that these agencies can effectively influence policy deliberation if they so choose. Unfortunately, except for this instance when their authority was directly challenged, they have not shown enthusiasm for such involvement. In fact, it was into the 1970s before a few of the larger SEAs assigned staff members to monitor Congress and present SEA views before that body.

Most SEAs are hard-pressed just to improve their effectiveness at the implementation stage of policy-making, where administrative rule-making can significantly modify the intent of laws. At times, SEA officials sit on panels to provide advice to OE as it establishes administrative guidelines for federal programs. The more aggressive SEAs sometimes establish state-level guidelines that go beyond those devised by OE. Occasionally, such initiatives are reflected in subsequent federal guidelines. When this does happen, as Elazar notes, the effect can well be to extend "the powers of the states in shared programs even beyond those actually authorized by congressional legislation and inference."[1]

On balance though, SEA policy-making initiatives, even at the implementation stage, are relatively infrequent. Such abstinence is a luxury SEAs can ill afford given that, at the federal level, Congress passes highly categorical laws and OE devises restrictive guidelines while at the state level, legislatures and governors are increasingly inclined to put additional constraints on the freedom of SEAs to administer federal programs. In short, the inability or unwillingness of SEAs to participate in federal policy-making has probably carried with it high costs.

Many SEA officials seem to be overwhelmed by the massive and swift federal initiative in educational governance. Having long been assigned stewardship over a well-defined but minimal set of regulatory activities they were not prepared for the dramatically different response required. In retrospect, the administrative patterns established over the years before the recent federal interventions may well be the major cause for their lack of responsiveness to the changing policy-making situation. During those quieter days they acted defensively rather than aggressively, placated rather than innovated, and in general, sought tranquility in carrying out assigned tasks. They became insecure as conditions changed and retreated in the comfort of established, even though inappropriate, patterns of management.

SEAs and Federal Programs: A Systems View

The discussion regarding the impact of federal aid on SEAs and the responses devised by these agencies has been framed in a systems perspective. This perspective includes the input demands and resources that have acted as stimuli for action, the SEAs' intraorganizational thruput responses that have focused on tasks, the complementary thruput activity of interorganizational relations, the outputs derived, and, finally, feedback of these outputs to those who initiated efforts by making demands and providing resources. This perspective, which is represented in Figure 15, will be used to organize discussion for the remainder of the chapter.

Inputs: Demands and Resources

Organizations, whether in the private sector or in the public sector, exist to provide need satisfaction. SEAs were founded as the states' nineteenth-century response to the need to monitor state fiscal resources set aside for school districts. Until recently most SEAs remained small and narrow in the scope of their activities. While state legislatures held down state-level resource inputs for education, state-level policy makers felt little urgency to increase the SEAs' staffs or the scope of their activities.

This situation has changed dramatically and most states have accepted a greater responsibility for provision of resources for schools. As the states expanded their role in educational governance, SEAs were called upon to upgrade their ability to regulate school-district activity. However, the states' demands and resources grew at a relatively steady pace. When the federal government's input expanded with such programs as the NDEA and the ESEA, SEAs were challenged as never before. Federal funds came to the states in the form of highly specific categorical grants and required the SEAs to plan and carry out diverse tasks. Congress, perhaps more than state legislatures, recognized the need to upgrade the SEAs' capacity to meet these expanding demands and set aside funds for the administration of federal programs. In fact, in many SEAs the dramatic expansion of staff during the 1960s and into the 1970s was due almost totally to federal resource inputs.

A major problem for SEAs is that there were debilitating features associated with these substantial resource inputs. Federal funding practices have created a high level of uncertainty for SEA program directors.* Administrative tasks remain constant, or even increase in scope once long-range plans are made, but federal resources, which are often approved after programs have actually begun, tend to vary up and down annually because of the state of the

---

*There is some indication that this problem may be alleviated in the future. The ESEA, as revised and approved by Congress in late 1974, included several key provisions that should go a long way toward relieving the uncertainties associated with federal aid that disturb SEA and school district administrators. These provisions include a four-year extension to the life of the program, a guarantee of at least 85% of fiscal 1974 funding for districts, and a consolidation of major portions of NDEA Title III and ESEA Title II library programs.

FIGURE 15. SEAS AND THE IMPLEMENTATION OF FEDERAL PROGRAMS: A SYSTEMS VIEW

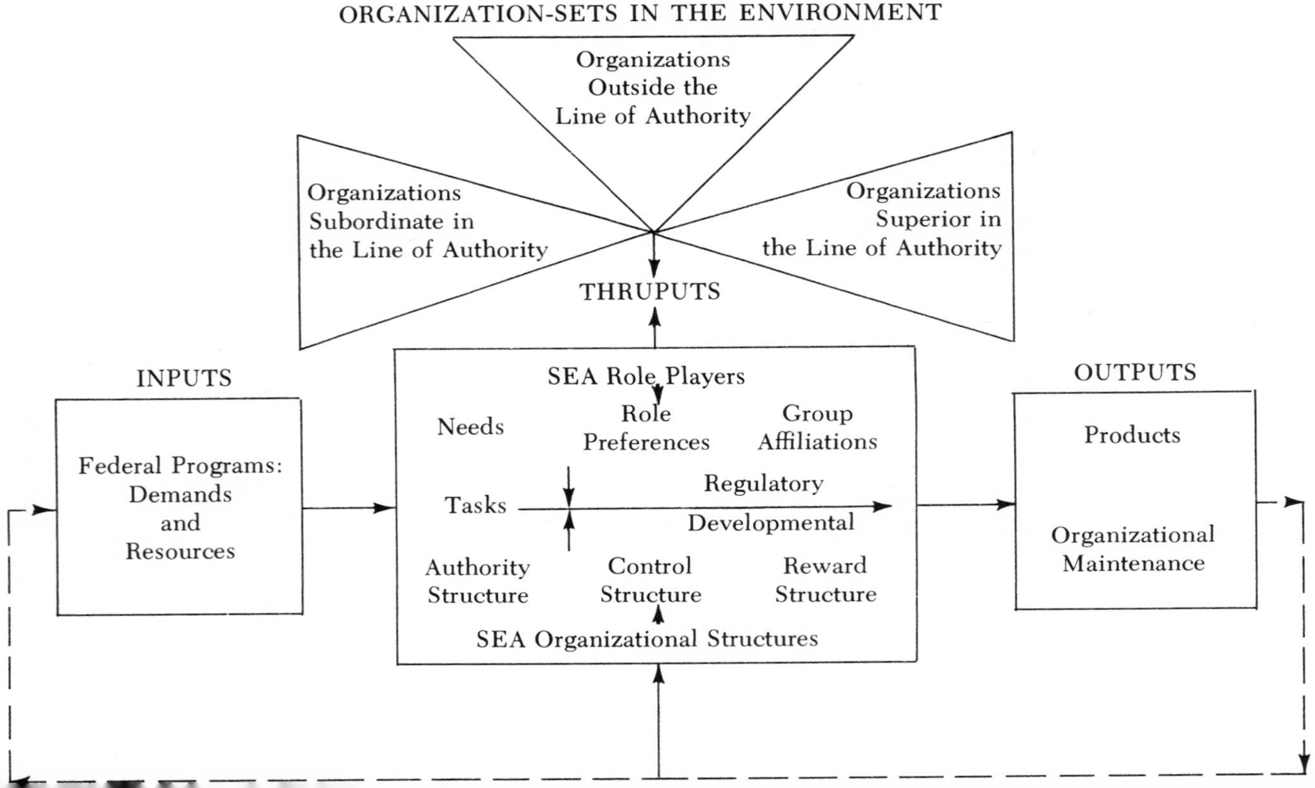

ORGANIZATION-SETS IN THE ENVIRONMENT

Organizations Superior in the Line of Authority

Organizations Outside the Line of Authority

Organizations Subordinate in the Line of Authority

THRUPUTS

SEA Role Players

Role Preferences

Group Affiliations

Regulatory

Developmental

Needs

Tasks

Authority Structure

Control Structure

Reward Structure

SEA Organizational Structures

INPUTS

Federal Programs: Demands and Resources

OUTPUTS

Products

Organizational Maintenance

economy, congressional budgetary practices, and occasional executive branch refusal to release funds already approved by Congress.* Such federal practices cause many SEA administrators to proceed with understandable caution.

Once federal funds finally reach the state level, SEA officials must be alert to possible encroachments by state legislatures and governors and their monitoring agencies. There is an increasing tendency on the part of legislatures to put state-level restrictions on SEA administrative practices concerning federally funded programs. Governors, for their part, are wary of permitting executive divisions to gain too much independence of action. As a result, SEA organizational structures may be dictated by statute, personnel recruitment may be severely limited by restrictive civil service or personnel board rulings, and space for housing new programs may be inadequate or nonexistent.

SEA officials compound these resource-input limitations when they continue to recruit staff from among their in-state, rural-school-district friends to administer federal programs. Such personnel tend to resist change and prefer not to place extensive demands on district administrators. In addition, they are often held in low esteem by urban-school-district administrators with whom they must work, a special problem with the massive ESEA Title I program. Although SEAs can do little about poor salary structures or the insecurities attached to federal program administration, they could at least make an effort to recruit from different sources. As a recent OE survey has established, "Given the need for managerial and technical talent . . . and the increasing pool of unemployed professionals (such as engineers and aerospace talent), there are implications for and possibilities of moving more technology into education and government."[2]

Thruputs

With demand established and resources garnered, SEAs must get on with the regulatory and developmental tasks at hand. The staff members who are to accomplish these tasks have to be accommodated in appropr ate organizational structures. In addition, agency

---

*An extreme example of this practice occurred when the Nixon Administration impounded about $1 billion already committed to educational programs by Congress for fiscal year 1973. This action was challenged in the courts and as a result the funds withheld were to be released over a period of several years. However, school districts and SEAs that counted on these resources for their 1973 budgets were forced to drop programs or find alternative sources of funding.

leaders have to establish and maintain satisfactory relations with other organizations that can support the attainment of tasks. These are all elements of the thruput process.

TASKS: REGULATION AND DEVELOPMENT. SEAs pursue *regulatory* tasks to ensure that school districts comply with the intent of laws, rules, regulations, and guidelines. That is, as monitoring agencies, SEAs try to assure policy makers at both the state and the federal level that resources provided to school districts are, in fact, focused on the achievement of intended outcomes. Regulatory activities, such as the auditing of school district expenditures, have been the responsibility of SEAs since the states began to contribute to the support of elementary and secondary education.

The addition of federal program regulatory activity has required SEAs not only to do more of the same, but to do new things. In many instances this has created difficulties. Evaluation, for example, has become a major concern since recent federal programs were inaugurated, but many SEA officials have had little formal training in evaluation techniques. In addition, because SEA officials are recruited from among school district administrators, they usually have established collegial relationships with those whom they are supposed to evaluate and they hesitate to monitor compliance of their friends very stringently. Of course, the ineffectiveness of OE's efforts to support SEAs that do attempt to enforce program intent does not help the situation either.

Developmental tasks, such as goal setting and planning, have enabled some SEAs to set future policy directions for education in their states. Most SEAs had neither the mandate nor the fiscal and human resources to pursue this function prior to the passage of such federal programs as the NDEA and the ESEA. Once federal resources became available the need for SEAs (and school districts) to plan, gather information about educational needs, and establish statewide priorities became unavoidable.

It was only in the mid 1970s, and then only in a handful of SEAs, that responses to the challenge began to emerge. For the main part SEAs have only minimally increased their own commitment to planning (from 5.2% to 8.4% of total SEA resources between 1966 and 1970).[3] Neither have they applied ESEA Title V funds, which are explicitly aimed at improving the SEAs' ability to plan and set goals (25% of these funds were committed to planning in 1966 and the commitment actually decreased to 16% in 1970).[4] In most instances the planning that does occur takes place at the program-unit level, not at the top level of SEAs.

No doubt the situation could be improved if Congress did away with such constraining practices as late funding and overly specified programs and committed itself to the need for better planning to the point that it provide planning funds to help SEAs and school districts prepare *before* the actual implementation of programs. State legislatures could also facilitate SEA preparation for federal program administration when federal resources are slow in reaching the state level by advancing state planning funds on a temporary loan basis. But unless SEA management practices are modified, it is unlikely that any such federal or state modifications would have a lasting effect. What seems to be required is a greater commitment to planning by top-level SEA officials. More and better qualified planners will have to be secured, put on permanent state appointments, and given sufficient authority so they can influence overall agency planning efforts. If such persons cannot be secured because of state-level constraints, then at least planning specialists, on a consulting basis, can be brought in to help SEAs establish planning designs and run in-service training courses for top-level officers who will be responsible for managing them.

Role Players. Results of SEA administration of federal programs such as the ESEA and the NDEA vary, often even across programs *within* single agencies. A good deal of the variation is due to differences in career needs, role dispositions, and group affiliations of SEA staff members.

CAREER NEEDS. SEAs attract several different types of staff members who, as might be expected, have different and sometimes conflicting needs. SEAs are sometimes accused of providing a safe haven for superintendents nearing the ends of their careers. There are at least some former superintendents to be found among most SEA staffs, a good many of whom try to pattern their work to maximize tranquility and security. But there are others who have different needs. Either because they are saddled with low pay scales or because they desire to infuse new ideas, SEAs also recruit young and relatively inexperienced staff members. Interested in establishing themselves in their new careers, they can be expected to be highly motivated and to seek recognition for their accomplishments. To complicate matters there are some educators midway through their careers and a few others who have moved into SEAs from other governmental agencies or from private industry. Many of these staff members either hold, or hope to attain, high office in their SEAs so they will likely view matters differently than either the near-retirement group or the young and inexperienced group.

ROLE DISPOSITIONS. There are two identifiable administrative styles among SEA staff members. The most predominant style is that of the SEA officials who feel their role is to support school districts. Such staff members prefer to permit school district officials maximum discretion concerning federal program administration and resist "policing" them when they deviate from program intent. The other style is that of the content-oriented officials who specialize in, for example, evaluation, curriculum, or finances. Relatively few in number, these staff members tend to be more aggressive when they work with school district personnel and insist on compliance, even if this results in strained SEA–school-district relations.

As might be expected, these groups are often in conflict. Those who think program accomplishment is most important are viewed by those who stress collegial relations as a threat to the continuity of the states' educational well-being. Conversely, program-oriented personnel think that district-oriented staff retard improvement of educational performance. SEA inability to co-ordinate program activities to accomplish system-wide objectives is directly related to the fact that these groups find it difficult to cooperate.

GROUP AFFILIATIONS. We have already noted two ways of grouping SEA staff. The first, based on point-in-career, divides SEA groups according to former superintendents, young and inexperienced staff members, and mid-level career officers and those few staff members who are recruited, because of their experiences, from outside of educational organizations. The second is based on school-district *vs.* program orientation. These are crossed over by a third grouping: the length of service in SEAs, which varies from those who date back to quieter times before the federal interventions of the 1960s, those who were recruited during the hectic years of greatest SEA expansion, and those who were hired during the early 1970s while SEAs tried to consolidate. The several elements of group affiliation—point-in-career, role orientation, and length of service—make personnel management in the SEAs a most challenging experience.

Organizational Structures. The cement that brings staff members and tasks together is composed of a mixture of authority, control, and reward structures. These formal organizational structures function to see that demands are satisfied and staff members are disposed to remain and perform required tasks. However, structures that are effective at one time may not be effective at another time. SEAs performed a relatively stable set of tasks until their administrative responsibilities expanded dramatically with increased state and federal inputs. The SEAs were challenged as never before to modify their organizational structures to meet these changing demands.

Perhaps the major structural challenge confronting SEAs is to maintain a semblance of agency-wide co-ordination while they take on administration of categorical programs that require concentrated effort. A myriad of program tasks has been added to the relatively simple auditing and record-keeping tasks associated with state aid formulas. The level of stress that emanates from this co-ordination *vs.* concentration dilemma is highly contingent upon SEA ability to modify authority, control, and reward structures to meet changing demands.

AUTHORITY STRUCTURES. SEA leaders try to devise authority structures that reduce uncertainty, assure equitable allocation of resources, and in general, facilitate task accomplishment. The structural responses of SEAs to the introduction of federal programs have varied from dividing federal programs among existing units to establishing new units to oversee all aspects of individual programs. The first enhances agency-wide co-ordination of effort, but often at the cost of not achieving program objectives. The second promotes achievement of program objectives, but probably, by creating separate interest groups, at the cost of debilitating agency-wide co-ordination of efforts.

A structural response that lies somewhere between these two extremes is to divide programmatic tasks among existing units but establish a separate office to co-ordinate activities of the various units involved in the program. The intent is to insure that program objectives will be served while the staff involved still identify with wider SEA purposes. In practice, however, it is difficult for a co-ordinating office to get such staff to focus on program requirements on a continuing basis; because they are assigned to federal programs on a part-time basis other demands that require their attention often must take priority. Even if these staff members work to devote more time to federal programs, they are still under pressure to constrain participation by their primary-unit superiors who, understandably, are concerned about fulfilling their own unit's task requirements. In short, whichever structural response an SEA chooses to make, it will encounter problems.

CONTROL STRUCTURES. With the growth in federal aid, tasks have become more complex, new units have proliferated, staffs have grown, and relations with school districts have intensified. The more complex and differentiated the SEAs become, the more necessary it is to establish and maintain control structures such as policies and administrative guidelines laid down by state boards that assure co-ordination of the subsystems.

As a result SEA administrators spend much of their time attending meetings and creating flurries of paper as they try to codify agency responses to federal program needs. Whether the outcome has been worth the effort is questionable. Most SEAs still produce different sets of guidelines and application forms for different federal programs. Only a few have even attempted to monitor diverse program activities by establishing co-ordinating groups that cut across separate bureaus and divisions or by reviewing federal programs at the level of the state superintendent or his immediate lieutenants. When monitoring is conducted, it often is not vigorously pursued. For example, even where ESEA Title V projects are administered by the state superintendent's office, they are rarely linked together to facilitate SEA-wide planning. Finally, most SEAs do not appear to have master plans for the administration of federal programs. Some programs are shared among existing units, some are given separate status as bureaus, and others are accorded separate status as divisions. The outcome is that lines of reporting are often confused and differences in organizational rank between program directors hinder exchange of information. Until SEAs achieve a better conception of their overall direction, it will be extremely difficult for them to establish control structures that can adequately account for necessary relations across individual programs.

REWARD STRUCTURES. SEA leaders devise reward strategies to enhance their staffs' ability to serve agency-determined priorities. The inability of SEAs to attract and retain sufficient numbers of well-qualified staff members indicates that the response to this need has not been sufficient. Some problems appear to be beyond their immediate control. For example, it is difficult for them to overcome the problems caused by late federal funding, fluctuations in program-funding levels, encroachments by state legislatures on their administrative prerogatives, and civil service restrictions on hiring and promotion practices.

Still there are inadequate intraorganizational practices that can be ameliorated. SEAs still do not seem to have been able to instill in their staffs a sense of overall agency mission. Program directors are not prone to co-ordinate activities across unit lines when there are no organizational rewards for such co-ordination. On the contrary, they actively pursue independent lines of action because they feel that rewards (such as promotion in their SEAs or recruitment by other organizations such as OE and school districts) will only be granted if they establish exceptional program records.

Relationships with Other Organizations. To achieve their purposes SEAs must convince the organizations they work with to provide resources, carry out tasks, and value agency outputs. The federal government's intervention in education has required SEAs to put more emphasis on interorganizational relations. Established relations have been modified and new ones have been developed. In the past SEAs only related on a continuing basis with the subordinate organizations they regulate and the superordinate organizations to which they were responsible. Expansion of the federal role has not only resulted in new and complex interactions with Congress and OE, but also with other education-related organizations that have a stake in federal program outcomes.

Because these organization-sets are not susceptible to internal bureaucratic controls and rewards, SEAs have had to rely on alternative influencing mechanisms to gain their cooperation: *reward* when benefits accrue from cooperation; *coercion* when losses occur from refusal to cooperate; *expertness* when one organization possesses special knowledge that other organizations require; *legitimacy* when contracts or other authoritative and formal agreements require organizations to work together; and *identification* when organizations view association for the sake of association as desirable.

The SEAs' use of these influencing mechanisms is dependent on three factors. The first is the need to *recognize* that interacting is important. For the organization-sets that are superior and subordinate, with the possible exception of Congress, the SEAs fully recognize this necessity. There have been far fewer interactions with the organization-set outside the line of authority. These organizations, most of which have only recently emerged as pertinent to SEA task accomplishment, have not actively sought contacts. SEA leaders, for their part, have not made great efforts to devise effective strategies for dealing with these outside organizations. There will probably be increasing pressure for such relationships in coming years given the inclination of organizations superior in the line of authority to press for greater accountability by enforcement agencies.

The second factor is how available *influencing mechanisms* are to the several parties. SEAs are at a disadvantage in relating to the superordinate organizations. Besides being able to tap an extensive reservoir of rewards and penalties, these organizations have begun to develop their own sources of information, thus neutralizing the expert-status advantage that SEAs long possessed. In contrast, SEAs have advantages over subordinate organizations because the SEAs can dispense or withhold substantial resources and because they possess up-to-date information regarding federal program requirements. In relating to outside organizations there are no such clear patterns. Rights and obligations are not so clearly defined as they are with the other two organization-sets.

The third is that the outcomes of interorganizational relations are, to a large extent, determined by the *skill* with which available influencing mechanisms are mobilized. SEA leaders have not done well in this regard. At the federal level, they lack the experience of OE officials and congressmen and their staffs, who are intimately familiar with the dynamics of federal policy-making. Similarly, they have not been very effective in fending off interventions by state legislatures and governors offices, both of which show an increasing interest in the internal affairs of SEAs. Their traditional collegial relations with district administrators have constrained SEA officials from instituting stringent regulatory controls.

SEAs have not been able to devise consistent and effective methods of working with an organizational environment that is expanding and less controllable than in the past. Therefore there is greater need for SEAs to improve their interorganizational effectiveness and there are indications that this can happen. Their ability to influence at the federal level was demonstrated when they secured a major SEA decision-making role for ESEA Title III. At the state level, infrequent but successful SEA efforts to establish special categories for hiring, remunerating, and promoting personnel provides a comparable example. Their potential to influence school districts can be significant; rule-making prerogatives, such as state-level guidelines, are employed by aggressive SEAs to move school districts to accomplish preferred outcomes. Finally, they can adapt to changing needs and expand their interactions with organizations outside the line of authority, as some agencies demonstrated when they brought private schools into the ESEA decision-making and resource-allocation pattern. But in the long run, internal SEA cohesion and goal setting must be achieved before these agencies can do much about their external relations problems. That is, overall agency goals must be delineated and agreed upon to provide a basis for deciding which organizations are relevant and what strategies are appropriate in relating to them.

Outputs

The *raison d'être* of formal organizations is to produce valued outputs. If their products are regarded as insufficient, demands will increase and further resources will be put in jeopardy. In addition, an organization's leaders must give due consideration to a second output, organizational maintenance, to insure that its staff members will continue to process demands. At times these two output requirements are in conflict. Demands by resource providers may be viewed as too great by staff members. Similarly the staff's preferences may be in opposition to the provider's preferences.* Somehow, SEA leaders must establish a balance between production and organizational maintenance.

Products. A major difficulty for SEAs is that there are different perceptions of what they are supposed to produce. Congress provides resources to satisfy demands defined at the national level but state legislatures provide resources to satisfy demands set at the state level. When their definition of demands varies from that of Congress, state-level policy-makers may conclude that the federal role played by SEAs skews agency efforts in inappropriate directions. Often SEAs become a battle field upon which such differences are contested, especially where state legislatures and gover-

---

*For example, the energy crisis, which received public recognition in the fall of 1973, led to demands for small and efficient automobiles. The auto industry, long geared to the production of large, and perhaps, purposefully uneconomical cars, found it difficult to adjust to this changing environmental demand.

nors have taken the initiative to establish educational programs. To complicate matters, school districts have their own program preferences and may expect SEAs to support them, even if these preferences run counter to the expectations of state or federal policy-makers. In short, how well SEAs are judged in their productivity regarding federal programs is at least partially dependent upon who is making the judgment.

Internal factors, such as administrators' preferences and the skilled manpower available, have also contributed to the criticism of SEA effectiveness in regulating school district compliance with federal intent, evaluating program outcomes, and developing state-level goals and long-range plans. Many SEA administrators appear committed to maintaining good relations with school district administrators, even if this means compromising demands established by federal and state law. Furthermore, so long as the major criteria for SEA personnel appointment is their acceptability to local school people, they will probably lack the specialized skills required to achieve outputs.

Organizational Maintenance. If their staff members do not fulfill their tasks the ability of SEAs to respond to demands and achieve organizational ends will be severely reduced. The SEA staffs will make the effort if they view their leaders as supportive, their work loads as tolerable, and the program objectives as clear and appropriate. These maintenance issues are as critical beyond the SEAs' boundaries as they are within them because these agencies rely on school districts to carry out assigned tasks.

In the past when SEA tasks were relatively constant, maintenance requirements were not too difficult to satisfy, but with the impact of federal programs they increased dramatically. SEA staffs have, on the average, more than doubled, creating need for intraorganizational accommodations. Furthermore, SEAs have been hard-pressed to maintain good relations with school districts because of the demands of federal programs. These rapidly changing internal and external situations have caused enormous difficulties for top-level SEA officials. High turnover rates among SEA staffs and school district resistance to stringent guidelines indicate that dissatisfactions are real. If SEA leaders are unable to surmount these problems, self-perpetuating crises may be created. If SEA staff are unhappy because of their role definitions or because they believe their work loads to be excessive, they can refuse to perform as expected or leave the organization. School district officials who are unhappy with SEA performance can sabotage their efforts by minimal compliance or by petitioning state legislators or congressmen to intervene on their behalf.

Feedback

State and federal policy-makers will eventually judge how well SEAs meet their expectations. If they are relatively satisfied with SEA products they will, in all probability, continue to provide resources. On the other hand, if they are sufficiently dissatisfied with agency products they will probably increase demands and/or reduce subsequent resource inputs. Of course, one of the SEAs' difficulties is that they are highly dependent on how effectively school districts go about implementing programs that are intended to fulfill these expectations. There are indications that dissatisfied resource providers will be demanding greater SEA accountability. Many state legislatures are looking closely at SEA activities. Some are actually passing legislation that mandates program objectives and administrative structures. Congress, in its more recent statutes, has stipulated similarly detailed and stringent requirements with which SEAs must comply, including limitations on program management and evaluation. In fact, at least for a time, Congress actually denied the SEAs a role in the administration of a major federal program, ESEA Title III.

SEAs, like other organizations, attempt to obtain preliminary feedback so they can modify unpopular or ineffective practices *before* resource providers become irrevocably dissatisfied, but their feedback efforts could be improved. At minimum they could (1) pay closer attention to the moods of Congress; (2) be more receptive to OE's calls for SEA participation in setting directions for federal programs; (3) keep state legislators and governors better informed about federal program shifts and expected agency responses to these shifts; (4) make more frequent visits to school districts to get a clearer impression of what is actually being done; and (5) devise better means of obtaining and sharing information across their own subunits.

In Closing

The federal government has established a firm and continuing role for itself in the educational policy-making process. Educators at both state and local levels will henceforth have to give due consideration to the preferences and practices of federal policy-makers. However the federal role has not become pre-eminent. Fear of federal control is based more on myth than on reality.

Variations in responses to federal interventions indicate that the effect of federal grants is highly dependent on responses made at the state level. As Sharkansky has noted:

> One of the great ironies in Federal-state relations is that both ultraliberal critics of the state governments and ultraconservative advocates of states rights argue that Washington has more control over the states than is actually the case. For the liberal, the national government is responsible for much of what is good about the states. For the conservative the national government chokes any state efforts at individuality or creativity. Both partisans are wrong. There is much slippage in Washington's control over the grants-in-aid programs.[5]

The slippage has been duly noted by those SEAs that have seized upon the federal inputs as an opportunity to improve their internal capabilities. Other SEAs have not recognized this potential and, as a result, have viewed federal program administration as but another burden with which they must contend.

Challenges will increase for SEAs so long as the federal government uses education to achieve national purposes. Federal programs such as the NDEA and the ESEA do indeed affect the functioning of SEAs, but it appears clear that their impact is as dependent on the leadership displayed by these agencies as it is on federal laws, regulations, and guidelines.

The conditions under which SEAs function have changed significantly as a result of the federal impact. These enforcement agencies have been challenged to expand their role because they stand at the center of the educational policy-making process in the United States. As the National Academy of Education has concluded, what "they do and recommend can result in powerful leverage upon state legislative and gubernatorial policies affecting education throughout the state; can directly affect the functions and behaviors of local schools and school districts; and can frequently make or break the success of federal educational programs."[6] As the importance of their role has increased, those who provide resources are demanding that these agencies improve their ability to perform. Whether SEAs become more potent voices in the determination of educational decisions is dependent on their ability to grasp the initiative. Never before have these agencies been confronted with such problems or been presented with such challenging opportunities.

Notes

Chapter I

1. James D. Thompson, *Organizations in Action* (New York: McGraw-Hill Book Co., 1967), p. 159.
2. See Willis D. Hawley, "Dealing with Organizational Rigidity in Public Schools: A Theoretical Perspective," Paper read at the American Political Science Association Annual Meeting, 1972.
3. Frederick M. Wirt and Michael W. Kirst, *The Political Web of American Schools* (Boston: Little, Brown & Co., 1972), p. 112.
4. Edgar Fuller and Jim B. Pearson, eds., *Education in the States, Vols. I and II* (Washington, D.C.: National Education Association, 1969).
5. The reader interested in a detailed description of the early growth of SEAs should see Chapter III, "Emergence of State Educational Patterns," in Lee M. Thurston and William H. Roe, *State School Administration* (New York: Harper & Brothers, 1957).
6. *Analysis of the Budget Bill: 1957-58 Report of the Legislative Analyst* (Sacramento: California Legislature, 1957).
7. Burton Friedman, *State Government and Education: Management in the State Education Agency* (Chicago: Public Administration Service, 1971), pp. 16-17.
8. Morton Grodzins, "Centralization and Decentralization in the American Federal System," in R. A. Goldwin, ed., *A Nation of States* (Chicago: Rand McNally, 1963), pp. 3-4.
9. Jay D. Scribner, "Impact of Federal Programs on State Departments of Education," in Fuller and Pearson, *Education in the States, Vol. II*, p. 502.
10. Daniel J. Elazar, "The Shaping of Intergovernmental Relations in the Twentieth Century," in Daniel J. Elazar, ed., *The Politics of American Federalism* (Lexington, Mass.: D. C. Heath & Co., 1969), p. 20.
11. For an interesting treatment of federal-state relations in the nineteenth century see Daniel J. Elazar, *The American Partnership* (Chicago: University of Chicago Press, 1962); for a similar treatment of this topic in the twentieth century see Elazar, ed., *Politics of American Federalism*, pp. 20-30.
12. Roe L. Johns and Edgar Morphet, *Financing the Public Schools* (Englewood Cliffs: Prentice-Hall, 1960), p. 376.

13. For a most thorough review of the history of educational legislation at the federal level between 1945 and 1972, see *Education for a Nation* (Washington, D.C.: Congressional Quarterly, 1972), pp. 58-103.

14. For purposes of this work it is impossible to explore the dynamics of educational policy-making at the federal level in depth, particularly as forces are brought to bear on Congress to move proposals into legislation. The interested reader might want to review an excellent analysis of this process from the passage of the NDEA through the passage of the ESEA done by James L. Sundquist, *Politics and Policy: The Eisenhower, Kennedy and Johnson Years* (Washington, D.C.: The Brookings Institute, 1968). For the ESEA specifically, see the study by Stephen K. Bailey, *The Office of Education and the Education Act of 1965* (New York: Bobbs Merrill Co., 1966).

15. Johns and Morphet, *Financing the Public Schools*, p. 376.

16. Michael W. Kirst, "The Politics of Federal Aid to Education in California," in Joel S. Berke and Michael W. Kirst, *Federal Aid to Education* (Lexington, Mass.: D. C. Heath & Co., 1972), p. 61.

17. Norman Drachler, "Educational Futures and the Alternatives," Speech presented at U.S. Department of Health, Education, and Welfare Fair Luncheon, May 9, 1963.

18. Ewald B. Nyquist, "Emergent Functions and Operations of State Education Departments," Paper given at a conference on The Emerging Role of State Departments of Education with Implications for Vocational Education, Columbus, Ohio, February 27 to March 2, 1967.

19. Kirst, in Berke and Kirst, eds., *Federal Aid to Education*, p. 23.

20. U. S. Department of Health, Education, and Welfare, *State Departments of Education and Federal Programs*, Annual Report, Fiscal Year 1970 (Washington, D.C.: U.S. Government Printing Office, 1972), p. 10-11.

21. Advisory Council on State Departments of Education, *The State of State Departments of Education*, Fourth Annual Report (Washington, D.C.: U.S. Government Printing Office, 1969), p. 68.

22. *Analysis of the Budget Bill: 1970-1971 Report of the Legislative Analyst* (Sacramento: California Legislature, 1969), p. 234.

23. U. S. Department of Health, Education, and Welfare, Office of Education, Press Release, HEW-268, November 3, 1959.

24. U. S. H.E.W., *State Departments of Education*, pp. 10-11.

25. See Bailey, *Education Act of 1965*; Stephen K. Bailey and Edith K. Mosher, *ESEA: The Office of Education Administers a Law* (Syracuse: Syracuse University Press, 1968); and John Hughes and Anne D. Hughes, *Equal Education* (Bloomington: Indiana University Press, 1972).

26. Lawrence D. Haskew, "What Lies Ahead," in Edgar L. Morphet and David L. Jesser, eds., *Designing Education for the Future, No. 4* (New York: Citation Press, 1968), p. 45.

27. Friedman, *State Government and Education*, p. 34.

Notes to Chapter III 147

Chapter II

1. See Mike M. Milstein and Robert E. Jennings, *Educational Policy-Making and the State Legislature: The New York Experience* (New York: Praeger Publishers, 1973), pp. 8-10.

2. Advisory Council, *State Departments of Education,* Fourth Annual Report, p. 10.

3. William M. Evan, "The Organization-Set: Toward a Theory of Inter-Organizational Relations," in James D. Thompson, ed., *Approaches to Organizational Design* (Pittsburgh: University of Pittsburgh Press, 1966); and "A Systems Model of Organizational Climate," in Renato Tagiuri and George H. Litwin, eds., *Organizational Climate* (Boston: Graduate School of Business Management, Harvard University, 1968).

4. For a detailed history and analysis of the legislation and enactment of this program, see Hughes and Hughes, *Equal Education.*

5. Mike M. Milstein, "Functions of the California State Department of Education as they Relate to Two Federally Funded Programs" (Ph. D. diss., University of California at Berkeley, 1967).

6. Mike M. Milstein, "Federally Funded Educational Programs and State Education Agencies: A Comparative Case Study of State Level ESEA Administration in California and New York," Report to Improving State Leadership in Education, Denver, 1970.

7. Mike M. Milstein, "State Education Agency Planning and Federally Financed Programs: Perceptions of Selected Groups," Report to Improving State Leadership in Education, Denver, 1971.

8. Berke and Kirst, *Federal Aid to Education;* Jerome T. Murphy, "Title I of ESEA," *Harvard Educational Review,* vol. 41, no. 1 (February 1971), pp. 35-63; and Jerome T. Murphy, *Grease the Squeaky Wheel* (Cambridge: Center of Educational Policy Research, Harvard Graduate School of Education, 1973).

9. Berke and Kirst, *Federal Aid to Education,* p. xvi and p. 6.

Chapter III

1. Council of Chief State School Officers, *The State Department of Education,* rev. ed. (Washington, D.C., 1963), p. 10.

2. States such as Virginia that instituted state audits before federal audits were established are the exception that prove the rule: see Edith K. Mosher, "The Politics of Federal Aid to Education in Virginia," in Berke and Kirst, *Federal Aid to Education,* p. 308 *ff.*

3. For a similar conclusion, see Kirst, "Federal Aid to Public Education: Who Governs?" in Berke and Kirst, *Federal Aid to Education,* p. 63 *ff.*

4. U. S. Department of Health, Education, and Welfare, Office of Education, *Regulations and Guide, The National Defense Education Act, Title III, Section 141.6* (Washington, D.C.: Office of Education, 1958).

5. U. S. Department of Health, Education and Welfare, Office of Education, *NDEA Title III, Guidelines* (Washington, D.C.: U. S. Government Printing Office, 1965), p. 10.

6. U. S. Congress, Public Law 89-10, Section 205 (a) (5 & 6).

7. U. S. Department of Health, Education, and Welfare, Office of Education, *The First Year of Title I, Elementary and Secondary Education Act of 1965* (Washington, D.C.: Office of Education, 1966), p. 13.

8. Laurence Iannaccone, "The Politics of Federal Aid to Education in Massachusetts," in Berke and Kirst, *Federal Aid to Education,* p. 215.

9. See Hughes and Hughes, *Equal Education.*

10. Nyquist, "Functions and Operations of State Education Departments."

11. Murphy, "Title I of ESEA," p. 43.

12 Ibid., p. 45.

13. U. S. Department of Health, Education and Welfare, Office of Education, *State Departments of Education, State Boards of Education, and Chief State School Officers* (Washington, D.C.: U.S. Government Printing Office, 1973), p. 34.

14. Gordon M. Ambach, "Education Policy Formation and the Future: A View from the State Education Department," Paper read at the American Educational Research Association, Minneapolis, 1970.

15. U. S. H.E.W., O.E. *State Departments, Boards, and Chief School Officers,* p. 78-89.

16. *American Education,* April 1969, p. 2.

17. Bailey and Mosher, *Office of Education Administers a Law,* p. 195.

18. For example, see Donald W. Johnson, "The Dynamics of Educational Change," *Bulletin of the California State Department of Education* XXXII, no. 3 (September 1963).

19. Murphy, *Grease the Squeaky Wheel,* p. 12.

20. Ibid., p. 188.

21. Ibid., see esp. pp. 21-29 and 190-221.

22. U. S. H.E.W., O.E., *State Departments, Boards, and Chief School Officers,* pp. 16-19.

23. For a smiliar discussion concerning federal practices that hinder school district planning, see Kirst, in Berke and Kirst, *Federal Aid to Education,* pp. 42-43.

24. For one of the exceptions to the rule, see a report of the Colorado SEA's effort to establish a planning system: Byron W. Hansford," Planning in the Colorado Department of Education to Facilitate Improvements in Education" Report to Improving State Leadership in Education, Denver, 1970.

25. Sidney C. Sufrin, *Issues in Federal Aid to Education,* (Syracuse: Syracuse University Press, 1962), p. 41.
26. See Kirst, in Berke and Kirst, *Federal Aid to Education,* p. 67.
27. ERIC Clearinghouse on Educational Administration, "Linking School to State Education Departments," (University of Oregon, Eugene, 1970) p. 1.
28. Charles M. Nix, "Internal Planmaking in State Education Agencies," Report to Improving State Leadership in Education, Denver 1972, p. 20.
29. Ibid.
30. Mohammad A. A. Shami and Martin Hershkowitz, "Goals and Needs of Maryland Public Education" (Maryland State Department of Education, Baltimore, 1972).
31. Jay D. Scribner, "The Politics of Federal Aid to Education in Michigan," in Berke and Kirst, *Federal Aid to Education,* pp. 131 and 155.
32. Michigan Department of Education, "A Study of Educational Needs: ESEA Title III" (Michigan Department of Education, Lansing, 1969) and "Purposes and Procedures of the Michigan Assessment of Education: Assessment, Report Number One" (Michigan Department of Education, Lansing, 1969).
33. California State Legislature, Assembly Bill 430, 1970.
34. Henry M. Brickell, "Organizing New York State for Educational Change," (The University of the State of New York, State Education Department, Albany, 1961).
35. The University of the State of New York, The State Education Department, "Goals for Elementary, Secondary and Continuing Education in New York State," rev. ed. (mimeograph, Albany, November 1973).

Chapter IV

1. Roald F. Campbell and Tim L. Mazzoni, Jr., "Recommendations" in Roald F. Campbell and Tim L. Mazzoni, Jr., eds., *State Policy Making for the Public Schools: A Comparative Analysis,* (Columbus, Ohio: Educational Governance Project, 1974) p. 398.
2. David J. Kirby and Thomas A. Tollman, "Background and Career Patterns of State Department Personnel," in Roald F. Campbell, Gerald E. Sroufe, and Donald H. Layton, eds., *Strengthening State Departments of Education* (Chicago: Midwest Administration Center, University of Chicago, 1967), p. 39.
3. Gary V. Branson, "The Characteristics of Upper Level Administrators

in Departments of Education," in Campbell and Mazzoni, *State Policy Making*, p. 151.

4. Ibid., p. 177.
5. Ewald B. Nyquist, "State Organization and Responsibilities for Education," in Edgar L. Morphet and David L. Jesser, eds., "Emerging Designs for Education, Report to Improving State Leadership in Education," Denver, 1968, p. 147.
6. Murphy, *Grease the Squeaky Wheel*, p. 95.
7. Milstein, "Functions of the California SEA," p. 100.
8. John S. Gibson, *The Massachusetts Department of Education: Proposals for Progress in the '70's* (Medford, Mass: The Lincoln Filene Center for Citizenship and Public Affairs, Tufts University, 1970), p. 139, as quoted in Murphy, *Grease the Squeaky Wheel*, p. 303.
9. Murphy, *Grease the Squeaky Wheel*, p. 95.
10. See Kirst, "The Politics of Federal Aid to Education in Texas," in Berke and Kirst, *Federal Aid to Education*, pp. 251-252, regarding the Texas SEA's staff-retention problems.
11. Advisory Council, *State Departments of Education*, p. 10.
12. Murphy, *Grease the Squeaky Wheel*, p. 47.
13. National Education Association, *Staff Salaries, State Departments of Education, 1969-70* (Washington, D.C.: Research Division, The Association, 1970-R7) p. 7.
14. See Nix, "Internal Planmaking," for examples of such efforts.
15. U. S. H.E.W., *State Departments of Education*, p. 2.
16. Iannaccone, in Berke and Kirst, *Federal Aid to Education*, p. 208.
17. Kearn Alexander, "The Implications of the Dimensions of Educational Need for School Financing," in Roe L. Johns, Kearn Alexander, and Richard Rossmiller, eds., *Dimensions of Educational Need* (Gainesville, Florida: National Educational Finance Project, 1969), p. 211.
18. U. S. Department of Health, Education and Welfare, Office of Education and the Office of Economic Opportunity, *Education: An Answer to Poverty* (Washington, D.C.: U.S. Government Printing Office, 1966).
19. See Nix, "Internal Planmaking."
20. See, for example, National Advisory Council on Education of Disadvantaged Children, *Annual Report, 1973* (Washington, D.C.: U.S. Government Printing Office, 1973).
21. See Wirt, "The Politics of Federal Aid to Education in New York," in Berke and Kirst, *Federal Aid to Education*, p. 331.
22. See Kirst, "The Politics of Federal Aid to Education in California," in Berke and Kirst, *Federal Aid to Education*, p. 122.
23. Nix, "Internal Planmaking," p. 12.
24. Office of the California Legislative Analyst, "State Support for Public Education in California with Particular Reference to Financing Elementary Education" (Statement before Senate Committee on Finance

and Governmental Administration, Sacramento, December 14, 1966), p. 9.
25. Nix, "Internal Planmaking," p. 22.

Chapter V

1. Evan, "The Organization-Set," in Thompson, ed., *Approaches to Organizational Design;* and "A Systems Model of Organizational Climate," in Tagiuri and Litwin, eds., *Organizational Climate.*
2. For pioneering studies see; James D. Thompson and William J. McEwen, "Organizational Goals and Environment: Goal Setting as an Interaction Progress," *American Sociological Review* XXII (February 1958), pp. 23-31; Sol Levine and Paul E. White, "Exchange as a Conceptual Framework for the Study of Interorganizational Relationships," *Administrative Science Quarterly* vol. 5, (March 1961), p. 395-601; Eugene Litwak and Lydia Hylton, "Interorganizational Analysis: A Hypothesis on Co-ordinating Agencies," *Administrative Science Quarterly,* vol. 6 (1962), p. 395; and Burton R. Clark, "Interorganizational Patterns in Education," *Administrative Science Quarterly,* vol. 10 (September 1965), pp. 224-237.
3. The "Conference on Interorganizational Decision Making" held in Evanston, Illinois, was sponsored by NASA. The papers read at that conference are reported in Matthew Tuite, Roger Chisholm, and Michael Radnof, eds. *Interorganizational Decision Making* (Chicago: Aldine Publishing Co., 1972).
4. See Ludwig von Bertalanffy, *General Systems Theory* (New York: George Braziller, 1968).
5. Paul R. Lawrence and Jay W. Lorsch, *Developing Organizations: Diagnosis and Action* (Reading, Mass.: Addison-Wesley Publishing Co., 1969), p. 25.
6. Thompson and McEwen, "Organizational Goals and Environment."
7. Daniel Katz and Robert L. Kahn, *The Social Psychology of Organizations* (New York: John Wiley & Sons, 1966), p. 305.
8. Thompson and McEwen, "Organizational Goals and Environment," p. 25.
9. See Clark, "Interorganizational Patterns in Education."
10. James L. Heskett, "Interorganizational Problem Solving in a Channel of Distribution," in Tuite, Chisholm and Radnor, eds. *Interorganizational Decision Making,* pp. 144-146. John P. French Jr., and B. H. Raven, "The Bases of Social Power," in Dorwin Cartwright, ed., *Stud-*

ies in Social Power (Ann Arbor: Institute for Social Research, University of Michigan, 1959), pp. 150-167, earlier employed these power bases to analyze the ability of leaders to move small groups. The only difference is that French and Raven used the term "referent" power to mean what Heskett labels "identification" power.

11. Fuller and Pearson, *Education in the States, Vol. II*, p. 73.

12. California State Department of Education, "A Brief Summary of Public Education in the State of California," (Sacramento, mimeographed, April 1965).

13. Wirt, "The Politics of Federal Aid to Education in New York," in Berke and Kirst, *Federal Aid to Education*, p. 346.

14. Iannaccone, in Berke and Kirst, *Federal Aid to Education*, pp. 210-214.

15. Milstein, "Functions of the California SEA," p. 152

16. California State Department of Education, "State Plan for Financial Assistance for Strengthening of Instruction in Science, Mathematics and Modern Foreign Languages" under Section 301–304 inclusive of Title III of P.L. 85-864–amended, and Section 4.51–amended 1958 (mimeographed).

17. Iannaccone, in Berke and Kirst, *Federal Aid to Education*, p. 227.

18. Milstein, "Functions of the California SEA," p. 157.

19. Wirt, in Berke and Kirst, *Federal Aid to Education*, p. 345.

20. Milstein, "Functions of the California SEA," p. 153.

21. Iannaccone, in Berke and Kirst, *Federal Aid to Education*, p. 207.

22. For a more complete discussion of this problem, along with recommendations for improving SEA–urban-school-district relations, see J. B. Morgan, Cecil Golden, Robert Greer, and Maurice Dutton, *"Improving Co-operation Between State Education Agencies and Urban School Systems,"* Report to Improving State Leadership in Education, Denver, 1972, and for a report of one SEA's efforts in this area, see J. B. Morgan and Maurice Dutton, *A Case Study of Improving Relationships Between Urban School Districts and the Texas Education Agency* (Denver: Education Commission of the States, 1975).

23. Ercell I. Watson, "Urban Pressures on the State Education Agencies," in Kenneth H. Hansen, ed., *The Governance of State Education Systems: Pressures, Problems, Options*, Report of the 1972 Institute for Chief School Officers, Spokane, Washington, July 27-August 4, 1972, p. 142.

24. Charles O. Fitzwalter, *Patterns and Trends in State School System Developments* (Washington, D.C.: National Education Association, 1967).

25. California State Department of Educaton, *The Emerging Requirements for Effective Leadership for California Education* (Sacramento: California State Printing Office, 1964), pp. 49-50.

26. See for example, Troy V. McKelvey and William B. Harris, "The Board of Cooperative Educational Services Model," in Troy V. McKelvey, ed., *Metropolitan School Organization*, Vol. I (1973), pp. 112-135.
27. Wirt, in Berke and Kirst, *Federal Aid to Education*, p. 369.
28. For a study of SEA influence on school districts that resulted in similar conclusions, see David Colton, "The Influence of State Education Agencies," *Administrators Notebook*, vol. xv, no. 9 (May 1967).
29. Berke and Kirst, *Federal Aid to Education*, p. 404.
30. National Education Association, *Rankings of the States, 1971* (Washington: Research Division, The Association, 1971), pp. 48-49.
31. *Report of the Senate Fact Finding Committee on Education* (Sacramento: Senate of the State of California, 1967 General Session), p. 12.
32. U. S. H. E.W., *State Departments of Education*, pp. 10-11.
33. See the findings of Mike M. Milstein and Robert E. Jennings, *Educational Policy-Making and the State Legislature: The New York Experience* (New York: Praeger Publishers, 1973), concerning New York, pp. 52-54.
34. U. S. H.E.W., O.E., *State Departments, Boards, and Chief School Officers*, pp. 60-61.
35. See Gerald Sroufe, "Recruitment Processes and Composition of State Boards of Education," (Paper presented at American Educational Research Association, Chicago, 1969).
36 U. S. H.E.W., O.E., *State Departments, Boards, and Chef School Officers*, pp. 86-87.
37. c.f. Laurence Iannaccone, "The State and Educational Policy Formulation: Prospects for the Future," (Paper presented at American Educational Research Association, Chicago, 1969).
38. Milstein and Jennings, *Educational Policy-Making: New York;* Tom Wiley, "State Politics and Educational Policy: A View from the Profession," (Paper presented at American Educational Research Association, Chicago, 1969); and Lawrence J. Fahey, "The California Legislature and Educational Decision Making" (Doctoral diss., Claremont Graduate School, 1969).
39. Kirst, in Berke and Kirst, *Federal Aid to Education*, p. 83.
40. Wirt, in Berke and Kirst *Federal Aid to Education*, p. 332.
41. Bailey, *et. al., School Men and Politics: A Study of State Aid to Education in the Northeast,* (Syracuse: Syracuse University Press, 1962), p. 27.
42. Tim L. Mazzoni, Jr., "The Policy Making Influence of State Boards of Education," in Roald F. Campbell and Tim L. Mazzoni, Jr., eds., *State Policy Making for the Public Schools: A Comparative Analysis* (Columbus, Ohio: Educational Governance Project, 1974), pp. 40-59.
43. Ira Sharkansky, "Agency Requests, Gubernatorial Support and Budget Success in State Legislatures," in Richard I. Hofferbert and Ira Shar-

kansky, eds., *State and Urban Politics* (Boston: Little, Brown & Co., 1971) pp. 323-342; and Nathan Weiss and Robert Laudicina, "Executive Leadership and Political Innovation in New Jersey State Politics," *Urban Education,* Vol. IV (January 1972), pp. 333-347.

44. Robert E. Jennings, "Alternative Roles and Interagency Relationships of State Education Agencies in Comprehensive Statewide Planning," Report to Improving State Leadership in Education, Denver, 1971, p. 28.

45. H. Milton Patton, "State Planning," in the Council of State Governments, *The Book of States, 1974-1975* (Lexington, Kentucky: The Council, Vol. XX, 1974), pp. 439-442.

46. James B. Conant, *Shaping Educational Policy* (New York: McGraw-Hill Book Co., 1964).

47. For further discussion on the establishment of the commission, see Terry Sanford, *Storm Over the States,* (New York: McGraw-Hill Book Co., 1967), pp. 116-121.

48. Jay D. Scribner, "Impact of Federal Programs on State Departments of Education," in Fuller and Pearson, eds., *Education in the States, Vol. II,* p. 521.

49. Bailey, *Education Act of 1965,* and Bailey and Mosher, *The Office of Education Administers a Law.*

50. Murphy, "Title I of ESEA," pp. 41-42.

51. U. S. House of Representives, Committee on Education and Labor, Special Subcommittee on Education, *Hearings to Strengthen and Improve Programs of Assistance for Our Elementary and Secondary Schools,* 89th Cong. 2nd sess., 1966, p. 9.

52. Kirst, in Berke and Kirst, *Federal Aid to Education,* p. 25.

53. The average resource concentration in California during the first year of the Title I program was $255 per child as compared to the nationwide average expenditure of $119. U. S. Office of Education, *The First Year of Title I, Elementary and Secondary Education Act of 1965,* (Washington, D.C.: Office of Education, 1965) p. ix.

54. Wirt, in Berke and Kirst, *Federal Aid to Education,* pp. 328 and 366.

55. Murphy, "Title I of ESEA," p. 45.

56. Murphy, *Grease the Squeaky Wheel,* p. 39.

57. Berke and Kirst, *Federal Aid to Education.*

58. California State Constitution, Article IX, Section 8.

59. 330 U.S. 1, 18, 1947.

60. Iannacone, in Berke and Kirst, *Federal Aid to Education,* p. 212.

61. Michael D. Usdan, David Minar, and Emanuel Hurwitz, *Education and State Politics* (New York: Teachers College Press, Columbia University, 1969).

62. U. S. Senate, *Department of Labor, and Health, Education and Welfare, and Related Agencies Appropriation Bill,* 1974, Report No. 93-414, 93rd Congress, 1st Session, October 2, 1973, pp. 124-126.

63. John M. Thompson, ed., *Teachers, History, and NDEA Institutes 1965,* (New York: American Council of Learned Societies, 1966), p. 13.
64. *Reviews of National Policies for Education, United States* (Paris: Organization for Economic Co-operation and Development, 1971) p. 13.
65. Francis Keppel, "The Business Interest in Education," *Phi Delta Kappan,* xlviii, no. 5. (January 1967), p. 188.
66. For problems of teacher training for use of these packages see Francis Keppel, "New Relationships Between Education and Industry," *Public Administration Review,* vol. 30 (July/August 1970), pp. 353-359.
67. U. S. Congress, Joint Economic Committee, Subcommittee on Economic Progress, *Report on Automation and Technology in Education,* 89th Cong., 2nd Sess. 1966., p. 11.

Chapter VI

1. Daniel J. Elazar, *American Federalism: A View from the States* (New York: Thomas Y. Crowell Co., 1966), p. 147.
2. U. S. Department of Health, Education, and Welfare, Office of Education, *State Departments of Education,* p. 45.
3. U. S. Department of Health, Education and Welfare, *State Departments of Education,* p. 5.
4. Ibid.
5. Ira Sharkansky, *The Maligned States* (New York: McGraw-Hill Book Co., 1972), p. 105.
6. National Academy of Education, *Policy Making for American Public Schools* (Washington, D.C.: By the Academy, 1969), p. 12.

Bibliography

Alexander, Kearn. "The Implications of the Dimensions of Educational Need for School Financing. In Roe L. Johns, Kearn Alexander, and Richard Rossmiller, eds., *Dimensions of Educational Need*. Gainesville, Florida: National Educational Finance Project, 1969.

Ambach, Gordon M. "Education Policy Formation and the Future: A View from the State Education Department." Paper read at American Educational Research Association, Minneapolis, 1970.

Bailey, Stephen K.; Frost, Richard T.; Marsh, Paul E.; and Wood, Robert C. *School Men and Politics: A Study of State Aid to Education in the Northeast*. Syracuse: Syracuse University Press, 1962.

Bailey, Stephen K. *The Office of Education and the Education Act of 1965* (Inter-University Case Program # 106). New York: Bobbs-Merrill Co., 1966.

Bailey, Stephen K., and Mosher, Edith K. *ESEA: The Office of Education Administers a Law*. Syracuse: Syracuse University Press, 1968.

Berke, Joel S., and Kirst, Michael W., eds. *Federal Aid to Education*. Lexington, Mass.: Lexington Books, D.C. Heath & Co., 1972.

von Bertalanffy, Ludwig. *General Systems Theory*. New York: George Braziller, 1968.

Brickell, Henry M. *Organizing New York State for Educational Change*. Albany: The University of the State of New York, The State Education Department, 1961.

Campbell, Roald F., and Mazzoni, Tim L., Jr., eds. *State Policy Making for the Public Schools: A Comparative Analysis*. Columbus, Ohio: Educational Governance Project, 1974.

Campbell, Roald F., and Mazzoni, Tim L., Jr. *State Governance Models for the Public Schools*. Columbus, Ohio: Educational Governance Project, 1974.

Campbell, Roald F.; Sroufe, Gerald E.; and Layton, Donald H; eds. *Strengthening State Departments of Education*. Chicago: Midwest Administrative Center, University of Chicago, 1967.

Clark, Burton R. "Interorganizational Patterns in Education." *Administrative Science Quarterly,* Vol. 10 (September 1965): 224-237.

Colton, David. "The Influence of State Education Agencies." *Administrators Notebook,* vol. xv, no. 9 (May 1967).

Council of Chief State School Officers. *The State Department of Education,* rev. ed. Washington, D.C.: By the Council. 1963.

Conant, James Bryant. *Shaping Educational Policy.* New York: McGraw-Hill Book Co., 1964.

Dochterman, Clifford L., and Beshoar, Barron B. *Directions to Better Education.* Denver: Improving State Leadership in Education, 1970.

Drachler, Norman. "Educational Futures and the Alternatives." Speech presented at U.S. Department of Health, Education, and Welfare Fair Luncheon, May 9, 1973.

Elazer, Daniel J. *American Federalism: A View from the States.* New York: Thomas Y. Crowell Co., 1966.

————— *The American Partnership.* Chicago: University of Chicago Press, 1962.

————— *The Politics of American Federalism.* Lexington, Mass.: D.C. Heath & Co., 1969.

ERIC Clearing House on Educational Administration. *Linking School to State Education Departments.* Eugene: University of Oregon, 1970.

Evan, William M. "A Systems Model of Organizational Climate." In Renato Tagiuri and George H. Litwin, eds., *Organizational Climate.* Boston: Graduate School of Business Management, Harvard University, 1968.

————— "The Organization-Set: Toward a Theory of Inter-organizational Relations." In James D. Thompson, ed., *Approaches to Organizational Design.* Pittsburgh: University of Pittsburgh Press, 1966.

Fahey, Lawrence J. "The California Legislature and Educational Decision Making." Doctoral dissertation, Claremont Graduate School, 1969.

Fitzwalter, O. Charles. *Patterns and Trends in State School System Developments.* Washington, D.C.: National Education Association, 1967.

French, John P., Jr., and Raven, B. H. "The Bases of Social Power." In Dorwin Cartwright, ed., *Studies in Social Power.* Ann Arbor: Institute for Social Research, University of Michigan, 1959.

Friedman, Burton. *State Government and Education: Management in the State Education Agency.* Chicago: Public Administration Service, University of Chicago, 1971.

Fuller, Edgar, and Pearson, Jim B., eds. *Education in the States; Vol. 1: Historical Development and Outlook, Vol. II: Nationwide Development Since 1900.* Washington, D.C.: National Education Association, 1969.

Galbraith, Jay. *Designing Complex Organizations.* Reading, Mass.: Addison-Wesley Publishing Co., 1973.

Gibson, John S. *The Massachusetts Department of Education: Proposals for Progress in the '70's.* Medford Mass.: The Lincoln Filene Center for Citizenship and Public Affairs, Tufts University, 1970.

Grodzins, Morton. "Centralization and Decentralization in the American Federal System." In R. A. Goldwin, ed., *A Nation of States.* Chicago: Rand McNally, 1963.

Hansen, Kenneth H., and Jesser, David L. "Society, Education and State Education Agencies: Implications of Societal Changes." In Edgar L. Morphet, David L. Jesser, and Arthur P. Ludka, eds., *Emerging State*

Responsibilities for Education. Denver: Improving State Leadership in Education, 1970.

Hansford, Byron W. *Planning in the Colorado Department of Education to Facilitate Improvements in Education.* Denver: Improving State Leadership in Education, 1970.

Haskew, Lawrence D. "What Lies Ahead." In Edgar L. Morphet and David L. Jesser, eds., *Designing Education for the Future, No. 4.* New York: Citation Press, 1968.

Hawley, Willis D. "Dealing with Organizational Rigidity in Public Schools: A Theoretical Perspective." Paper read at the American Political Science Association Annual Meeting, Washington, D.C., 1972.

Heskett, James L. "Interorganizational Problem Solving in a Channel of Distribution," In Matthew Tuite, Roger Chisholm, and Michael Radnor, eds., *Interorganizational Decision Making.* Chicago: Aldine Publishing Co., 1972.

Hughes, John, and Hughes, Anne O. *Equal Education.* Bloomington: Indiana University Press, 1972.

Iannaccone, Laurence. "The State and Educational Policy Formulation: Prospects for the Future." Paper presented at American Educational Research Association, Chicago, 1969.

Jennings, Robert E. "Alternative Roles and Interagency Relationships of State Education Agencies in Comprehensive Statewide Planning." Report to Improving State Leadership in Education, Denver, 1971.

Johns, Roe L., and Morphet, Edgar L. *Financing the Public Schools.* Englewood Cliffs: Prentice-Hall, Inc. 1960.

Johnson, Donald W. "The Dynamics of Educational Change." *Bulletin of the California State Department of Education* XXXII, no. 3 (September 1963).

Katz, Daniel, and Kahn, Robert L. *The Social Psychology of Organizations.* New York: John Wiley & Sons, 1966.

Keppel, Francis. "The Business Interest in Education." *Phi Delta Kappan* XLVIII, no. 5 (January 1967): 186-190.

──────── "New Relationships Between Education and Industry." *Public Administration Review,* vol. 30 (July/August 1970): 353-359.

Kimbrough, Ralph B. "Education in the State Political Setting." In Kenneth H. Hansen, ed. *The Governance of State Education Systems: Pressures, Problems, Options.* Report of the 1972 Institute for Chief School Officers, Spokane, Washington, July 27 to August 4, 1972, pp. 3-24.

Kirst, Michael W. "The Growth and Limits of Federal Influence in Education." Occasional Papers in the Politics of Education, School of Education, Stanford University, 1972.

Lawrence, Paul R., and Lorsch, Jay W. *Developing Organizations: Diagnosis and Action.* Reading, Mass.: Addison-Wesley Publishing Co., 1969.

──────── "Differentiation and Integration in Complex Organizations." *Administrative Science Quarterly,* vol. 12 (June 1967): 1-47.

——————— *Organization and Environment.* Boston: Harvard Graduate
School of Business Administration, 1967.

Levine, Sol, and White, Paul E. "Exchange as a Conceptual Framework for
the Study of Interorganizational Relationships." *Administrative Science
Quarterly,* vol. 5 (March 1961): 583-601.

Litterer, Joseph A. *The Analysis of Organizations.* New York: John Wiley &
Sons, 1965.

Litwak, Eugene, and Hylton, Lydia F. "Interorganizational Analysis: A
Hypothesis on Co-ordinating Agencies." *Administrative Science Quarterly,* vol. 6 (March 1962): 395-420.

McKelvey, Troy V., and Harris, William B. "The Board of Co-operative
Educational Services Model." In Troy V. McKelvey, ed., *Metropolitan
School Organization,* vol. I (1973): 112-135.

Milstein, Mike M. "Federal Aid and State Education Agencies." *Administrator's Notebook,* vol. XVI (March 1968) No. 7.

——————— "Federally Funded Educational Programs and State Education
Agencies: A Comparative Case Study of State-level ESEA Administration
in California and New York." Report to Improving State Leadership in
Education, Denver, 1970.

———————,"Functions of the California State Department of Education as
They Relate to Two Federally Funded Educational Programs." Ph.D. dissertation, University of California at Berkeley, 1967,

——————— "State Education Agency Planning and Federally Funded Programs: Perceptions of Selected Groups." Report to Improving State Leadership in Education, Denver, 1971.

Milstein, Mike, M., and Belasco, James A., eds. *Educational Administration and the Behavioral Sciences: A Systems Perspective.* Boston: Allyn &
Bacon, 1973.

Milstein, Mike M., and Jennings, Robert E. *Educational Policy Making and
the State Legislature: The New York Experience.* New York: Praeger Publishers, 1973.

Morgan, J. B., and Dutton, Maurice. *A Case Study of Improving Relationships Between Urban School Districts and the Texas Education Agency."*
Denver: Education Commission of the States, 1975.

Morgan, J. B.; Golden, Cecil; Greer, Robert; and Dutton, Maurice. "Im-
proving Cooperation Between State Education Agencies and Urban
School Systems." Report to Improving State Leadership in Education,
Denver, 1972.

Morphet, Edgar L., and Jesser, David L., eds. "Emerging Designs for Education." Report to Improving State Leadership in Education, Denver,
1968.

Murphy, Jerome T. *Grease the Squeaky Wheel.* Cambridge: Center for Educational Policy Research, Harvard Graduate School of Education, 1973.

——————— "Title I of ESEA." *Harvard Educational Review,* vol. 41, no. 1
(February 1971): 35-63.

National Academy of Education. *Policy Making for American Public Schools.* Washington, D.C.: By the Academy, 1969.

National Advisory Côuncil on Education of Disadvantaged Children. *Annual Report 1973.* Washington, D.C.: By the Council, 1973.

Nix, Charles M. "Internal Planmaking in State Education Agencies." Report to Improving State Leadership in Education, Denver, 1972.

Nyquist, Ewald B. "Emergent Functions and Operation of State Education Departments." Paper presented at the Conference on the Emerging Role of State Departments of Education with Implications for Vocational Education, Columbus, Ohio, February 27 to March 2, 1967.

Organization for Economic Cooperation and Development. *Reviews of National Policies for Education, United States.* Paris: By the Organization, 1971.

Patton, H. Milton. "State Planning." In Council of State Governments, *The Book of the States, 1974-1975,* vol. XX. Lexington, Kentucky: By the Council, 1974.

Robinson, Donald W. "The USOE and Research in Education." *Phi Delta Kappan,* XLVIII, no. 1 (September 1966): 2-5.

Sanford, Terry. *Storm Over the States.* New York: McGraw-Hill Book Co., 1967.

Sharkansky, Ira. "Agency Requests, Gubernatorial Support and Budget Success in State Legislatures." In Richard I. Hofferbert and Ira Sharkansky, eds., *State and Urban Politics.* Boston: Little, Brown & Co., 1971.

————— *The Maligned States.* New York: McGraw-Hill Book Co., 1972.

Sroufe, Gerald. "Political Systems Analysis in Educational Administration: Can the Emperor be Clothed." Paper presented at the American Educational Research Association, Chicago, 1969.

————— "Recruitment Processes and Composition of State Boards of Education." Paper presented at the American Educational Research Association, Chicago, 1969.

————— "State School Board Members and Educational Policy." *Administrators Notebook,* XIX, no. 2 (October 1970).

Sufrin, Sidney C. *Issues in Federal Aid to Education.* Syracuse: Syracuse University Press, 1962.

Sundquist, James L. *Politics and Policy: The Eisenhower, Kennedy and Johnson Years.* Washington, D.C.: The Brookings Institute, 1968.

Thompson, James D., and McEwen, William J. "Organizational Goals and Environment: Goal-Setting as an Interaction Process." *American Sociological Review,* XXII (February 1958): 23-31.

Thompson, James D. *Organizations in Action.* New York: McGraw-Hill Book Co., 1967.

Thompson, John M., ed. *Teachers, History, and NDEA Institutes 1965.* New York: American Council of Learned Societies, 1966.

Thurston, Lee M., and Roe, William H. *State School Administration.* New York: Harper & Brothers, 1957.

Toffler, Alvin. *Future Shock.* New York: Random House, 1970.

Tuite, Matthew; Chisholm, Roger; and Radnof, Michael, eds. *Interorganizational Decision Making.* Chicago: Aldine Publishing Co., 1972.

Usdan, Michael D; Minar, David; and Hurwitz, Emanuel. *Education and State Politics.* New York: Teachers College Press, Columbia University, 1969.

Watson, Ercell I. "Urban Pressures on the State Education Agencies." In Kenneth H. Hansen, ed., *The Governance of State Education Systems: Pressures, Problems, Options.* Report of the 1972 Institute for Chief School Officers, Spokane, Washington, 1972, pp. 141-153.

Weiss, Nathan, and Laudicina, Robert. "Executive Leadership and Political Innovation in New Jersey State Politics." *Urban Education,* vol. IV, no. 4 (January 1970): 333-347.

Wiley, Tom. "State Politics and Educational Policy: A View from the Profession." Paper presented at the American Educational Research Association, 1969.

Wirt, Frederick M., and Kirst, Michael W. *The Political Web of American Schools.* Boston: Little, Brown & Co., 1972.

Government Documents

Advisory Council on State Departments of Education. *The State of State Departments of Education.* Fourth Annual Report. Washington, D.C.: U.S. Government Printing Office, 1969.

California Legislative Analyst. "State Support for Public Education in California with Particular Reference to Financing Elementary Education." Sacramento: Statement before Senate Committee on Finance and Governmental Administration, December 14, 1966.

California Legislature. *Analysis of the Budget Bill: 1970-1971 Report of the Legislative Analyst.* Sacramento: California Legislature, 1969.

California Senate. *Report of the Senate Fact Finding Committee on Education.* Sacramento: Senate of the State of California, 1967.

California State Department of Education. "A Brief Summary of Public Education in the State of California," Mimeograph, April 23, 1965.

———— *The Emerging Requirements for Effective Leadership for California Education.* Sacramento: California State Printing Office, 1964.

———— "State Plan for Financial Assistance for Strengthening of Instruction in Science, Mathematics and Modern Foreign Languages under Section 301-304 inclusive of Title III of P.L. 85-864-amended." Sacramento, 1958. Mimeographed.

Michigan Department of Education. *A Study of Educational Needs: ESEA Title III.* Lansing: Michigan Department of Education, 1969.

———— *Purposes and Procedures of the Michigan Assessment of Education: Assessment Report Number One.* Lansing: Michigan Department of Education, 1969.

National Education Association. *Rankings of the States, 1971.* Washington, D.C.: Research Division, The Association, 1971.
———— *Staff Salaries, State Departments of Education, 1969-70.* Washington, D.C.: Research Division, The Association, 1970.
Shami, Mohammad A. A., and Hershkowitz, Martin. *Goals and Needs of Maryland Public Education.* Baltimore: Maryland Department of Education, 1972.
U.S. Congress, Joint Economic Committee, Subcommittee on Economic Progress. *Report on Automation and Technology in Education.* 89th Congress, 2nd Session, 1966.
U.S. Department of Health, Education, and Welfare. *State Departments of Education and Federal Programs,* Annual Report, Fiscal Year 1970. Washington, D.C.: U.S. Government Printing Office, 1972.
U.S. Department of Health, Education, and Welfare, Office of Education. *The First Year of Title I, Elementary and Secondary Education Act of 1965.* Washington, D.C.: U.S. Office of Education, 1966.
————*NDEA Title III, Guidelines.* Washington, D.C.: U.S. Government Printing Office, 1965.
————*Regulations and Guide, The National Defense Education Act, Title III, Sections 301-304.* Washington, D.C.: U.S. Office of Education, 1958.
————*State Departments of Education, State Boards of Education, and Chief State School Officers.* Washington, D.C.: U.S. Government Printing Office, 1973.
U.S. Department of Health, Education, and Welfare, Office of Education and Office of Economic Opportunity. *Education: An Answer to Poverty.* Washington, D.C.: U.S. Government Printing Office, 1966.
U.S. House of Representatives, Committee on Education and Labor, Special Subcommittee on Education. *Hearings to Strengthen and Improve Programs of Assistance for our Elementary and Secondary Schools.* 89th Congress, 2nd Session, 1966.
U.S. Senate. *Departments of Labor, and Health, Education and Welfare, and Related Agencies Appropriation Bill,* 1974, Report No. 93-414. 93rd Congress, 1st Session, 1973.
The University of the State of New York, The State Education Department. *Goals for Elementary, Secondary and Continuing Education in New York State* (rev.). Albany, Mimeograph, November 1973.

Index